T0290097

Evaluating the Impact of Training and Institutional Development Programs

A Collaborative Approach

Suzanne Taschereau

The World Bank
Washington, D. C.

The Economic Development Institute (EDI) was established by the World Bank in 1955 to train officials concerned with development planning, policymaking, investment analysis, and project implementation in member developing countries. At present the substance of the EDI's work emphasizes macroeconomic and sectoral economic policy analysis. Through a variety of courses, seminars, and workshops, most of which are given overseas in cooperation with local institutions, the EDI seeks to sharpen analytical skills used in policy analysis and to broaden understanding of the experience of individual countries with economic development. Although the EDI's publications are designed to support its training activities, many are of interest to a much broader audience. EDI materials, including any findings, interpretations, and conclusions, are entirely those of the authors and should not be attributed in any manner to the World Bank, to its affiliated organizations, or to members of its Board of Executive Directors or the countries they represent.

Because of the informality of this series and to make the publication available with the least possible delay, the manuscript has not been edited as fully as would be the case with a more formal document, and the World Bank accepts no responsibility for errors. Some sources cited in this paper may be informal documents that are not readily available.

The complete backlist of publications from the World Bank is shown in the annual *Index of Publications*, which contains an alphabetical title list (with full ordering information) and indexes of subjects, authors, and countries and regions. The latest edition is available free of charge from the Distribution Unit, Office of the Publisher, The World Bank, 1818 H Street, N.W., Washington, D.C. 20433, U.S.A., or from Publications, Banque mondiale, 66, avenue d'Iéna, 75116 Paris, France.

Suzanne Taschereau is a consultant currently living in Ottawa, Canada.

Library of Congress Cataloging-in-Publication Data

Taschereau, Suzanne, 1950-
    Evaluating the impact of training and institutional development
programs : a collaborative approach / Suzanne Taschereau.
        p.   cm. — (EDI learning resources series, ISSN 1020-3842)
    Includes bibliographical references.
    ISBN 0-8213-3700-9
    1. Economic development projects—Management—Study and teaching
—Evaluation. 2. Economic assistance—Management—Study and
teaching—Evaluation.   I. Title.   II. Series.
HD75.9.T37 1997
338.9'0068—DC20
                                                    96-27810
                                                    CIP

Contents

Foreword

Increasingly, development agencies involved in training and their partner institutions have realized that their success should and will be gauged by the results of their interventions on the ground. Thus, they are paying more attention to evaluating training in general and training impacts in particular.

The cumulative experience of impact evaluations carried out by the Economic Development Institute (EDI), its partner institutions, and practitioners around the world demonstrates that involving decisionmakers and potential users of evaluation information in the various phases of the evaluation—including defining its purpose and objectives, developing key indicators of impact, collecting and interpreting data, and formulating recommendations—can lead to valid and useful evaluation results and contribute to organizational learning.

However, little practical guidance is available to decisionmakers and trainers on how to carry out collaborative impact evaluations of training and institutional development activities and programs in a way that will lead to meaningful results. I am pleased to introduce this manual, which was commissioned by EDI's New Products and Outreach Division and is now being published under the auspices of EDI's Evaluation Unit, to help fill that gap.

Impact evaluations can be a great source of organizational learning. EDI is committed to improving its training and institutional development interventions and to assisting its partner institutions that wish to embark on the path of organizational learning through, among other means, systematic, useful, and collaborative impact evaluations. We hope that this manual can help make that happen.

Vinod Thomas, Director
Economic Development Institute

Author's Note and Acknowledgments

In the late 1980s, when I carried out the first impact study of the Economic Development Institute's (EDI's) training programs on policy and institutional development, little literature on the subject was available. Many years and several impact evaluations later, EDI invited me to write this manual to help World Bank task managers and partner institutions in developing countries to design and implement collaborative approaches for carrying out evaluations.

This manual is intended for managers of training and institutional development programs. Its objective is to provide clear and practical advice for those who believe that systematic learning from practice should guide their future actions. Given the rapid acceleration in the pace of change and pressures for effective use of limited funds, institutions are placing more emphasis on enchancing quality through monitoring and ongoing evaluation. Although written with impact evaluations in mind, the manual provides practical advice on developing evaluation plans, designing questionnaires, conducting interviews, reporting findings, and so on.

This manual would not have been possible without the impetus and the energy given it by John Oxenham of EDI's New Products and Outreach Division. I thank him for the idea, his encouragement, and his support throughout this project. I also would like to express my sincere appreciation to the training managers and decisionmakers at EDI, the evaluation specialists in other World Bank departments, and the representatives from EDI partner training institutions in many countries who took the time to share their experience and views on impact evaluation of training and to make helpful suggestions for the manual. In addition to those already mentioned, I would particularly like to thank Emmanuel D'Silva, Violaine le Rouzic, Paud Murphy, Brian Ngo, Ray C. Rist, Elca Rosenberg, and Alexander H. ter Weele of EDI; Mark Baird, Jan de Weille, Patrick Grasso, George Lear, Dariush Malekpour, and Boon Thiong Tay from other World Bank departments; and Joan Corkery, European Centre for Development Policy Management, The Netherlands; Guo Jin Zhang, Coordinating Committee on Agricultural Sector Training Network, People's Republic of China; José R. Nagel, Instituto Interamericano de Cooperación para la Agricultura, Costa Rica; and R. M. N'gosso, African Development Bank Training Centre, Côte d'Ivoire.

I am particularly indebted to Armand Van Nimmen, whose clarity of purpose, openness to a collaborative approach, and unrelenting support were critical in producing several impact evaluations that were methodologically rigorous and useful for decisionmaking. Many of the insights and examples in this manual are derived from these impact evaluations. If a good conceptual framework is essential for rigorous and systematic evaluation practice, grounding this practice in the realities of development change is critical. As task manager and consultant to the Municipal Development Programme for Sub-Saharan Africa (Harare, Zimbabwe), I learned to appreciate the complexities of policy and institutional development change processes. I am grateful to Joseph L. M. Mugore, who taught me the art of asking thoughtful questions and how to work with institutions so that they take responsibility for their own learning and their own development.

Producing a thoughtful, well-designed, and readable manual requires a tremendous amount of time, inspiration, creativity, and attention to detail. I am grateful to Ray Rist, who reviewed the manual and improved it through substantive contributions on evaluation design and methodology; Sumana Dhar, who researched and constructed the running example of the evaluation conducted by EDI and its partner, the Foundation for Advanced Studies in International Development, Tokyo; and Alice Dowsett for her professional editing of this manual.

Suzanne Taschereau

1

Impact Evaluation: What Is It and Why Do It?

Training institutions and international agencies concerned with increasing the capacity and performance of developing country institutions are increasingly interested in going beyond evaluations that are limited to numbers of activities and participants, and reactions to end-of-activity questionnaires. While these are useful measures, for some purposes they are of little help in determining the extent to which the activities have affected performance in the workplace. Similarly, these measures do not indicate whether changes in participants' knowledge, skills, and attitudes as a result of the activities have had any short- or long-term development effects on institutions or on the people those institutions serve.

The training and institutional development activities the Economic Development Institute (EDI) and its partner institutions undertake are diverse. They include designing and delivering courses aimed at increasing participants' knowledge and skills, facilitating seminars to foster policy dialogue among senior policymakers and implementors from different ministries and different levels of government, providing technical assistance with strategic planning workshops and formulation of strategic plans, carrying out action research in support of policy dialogue and organizational development, and providing instructional materials and equipment.

A review of the evaluation literature, including the literature produced by training institutions and development agencies, reveals varying definitions of and approaches to evaluation practice.

In this manual, impact evaluation means assessment of the direct and indirect effects of activities and programs on individual, institutional, and sectoral performance and/or on policies and the consequences for the welfare of the larger community.

Policy and institutional development are long-term processes. Tracing the impacts of training and institutional activities to the furthest limits of change in society is rarely possible. Most impact evaluations of training and institutional development interventions, whether activities or programs, will therefore study the effects that can be identified as far as possible down the cause and effect sequence to which the institution contributes, and that can still be traced back to its interventions.

Impact evaluation can be distinguished from other types of evaluation by the area of the program upon which it will focus. This logic follows the evolution of the program as it unfolds and has been a generally useful paradigm in evaluation research. Rossi and Freeman (1993), for example, distinguish between three programs phases: conceptualization and design, monitoring and implementation, and assessment of effectiveness. Each of these phases is compatible with different evaluation strategies. At the conceptualization phase of the program, a diagnostic evaluation procedure may be appropriate, as research questions address program features such as the program's underlying assumptions, its logic, major stakeholders, the program's objective, and the context in which the implementation is to occur. Adequate understanding of these issues is critical before a program is designed and started.

> *This manual uses the Joint Training Program on Development Programming and Project Management of the Economic Development Institute and the Foundation for Advanced Studies on International Development (FASID), the Jazpanese partner, as a case study to illustrate the various aspects of a practical, collaborative approach to impact evaluation. The manual reviews the evaluation of the first six courses, which took place during 1991–93.*
>
> *The program consisted a series of courses, two to five weeks in length, geared to provide rigorous training in the analytical, planning, and management techniques required by both donors and recipients for the efficient selection, evaluation, and implementation of development projects and to help participants understand the economic, financial, political, and sectoral contexts within which projects are selected and implemented.*
>
> *The target participants were mainly government officials and private sector managers from developing countries and those in transition and Japanese government officials expected to be associated with Japan's program in development cooperation.*
>
> *An end-of-activity evaluation followed each course. As the planning and implementation of each course built on the experience of the preceding one, the task managers' assessment went beyond mere quantitative evaluation of the specific activity. Moreover, in 1994 EDI and FASID contracted two outside consultants to evaluate the effectiveness of all six courses. The consultants' reviews serve to illustrate how impact evaluation can be used to study whether training changed participants' skills and attitudes, and thus had any effects on their work.*

The second stage, monitoring and implementation, focuses on the program's operations after it has been started. Here, several types of evaluations may be appropriate for a given objective. These have been described as formative evaluation approaches by the U.S. General Accounting Office (GAO 1994), and are intended to improve the overall operations of the program. Several different evaluation types are included in this group. Evaluability assessment, which attempts to answer the basic question of whether a program can be evaluated, is included in this group. Perhaps best known in the process or implementation evaluation that focuses on the delivery of the treatment and assesses the program's conformity with its basic design. Performance monitoring is sometimes included in this group. This type of evaluation periodically reviews the short–term outcomes of the program, along with its quality, to assess the degree to which the program's activities affect these outcomes.

It is in the last program phase, the assessment phase, that we find impact evaluation. An impact evaluation assesses the extent to which a program has caused desired changes in the target audience. It implies a set of program objectives that can be identified and used as the basis for measuring the program's impact. Thus the overall goal of an impact evaluation is to determine if, and the extent to which, a program has met its objectives. In the assessment phase of the program distinguishing impact from the program's outputs and outcomes is often valuable. Outputs refer to the immediate consequences of the program, whereas outcomes describe more intermediate results. Both outputs and outcomes may be intended or unintended, and need to be assessed for their logical relationship to final program objectives. Often, time constraints make it difficult to wait for results from an impact evaluation. By assessing program outputs and outcomes, we are able to determine their logical consistency with final program objectives, and thereby demonstrate the likelihood of achieving these objectives in the absence of an impact evaluation study.

The GAO work cited previously classifies impact evaluation as a type of summative evaluation. With this general type of evaluation, the interest is in program results rather than its formation or operations. Included in this more general type of evaluation, along with impact evaluation, is evaluation synthesis. Evaluation synthesis attempts to analyze evaluation results from multiple programs or from sites within a program to determine if, at this more aggregate level, some program effect can be found. A number of methods can be and are used in evaluation synthesis, ranging from pooling data from multiple programs, to analyzing effect sizes across programs in a meta-analysis, and finally to using more qualitative methods. These methods attempt to overcome the limitations often imposed by assessing individual programs by using data and/or results from a number of often different, but similar evaluations.

In the specific area of evaluating training programs, Kirkpatrick (1975) describes four evaluation steps that provide much greater detail in assessing the results of these programs, including their impact. The four steps he describes—reaction, learning, behavior, and results—can be viewed as a continuum along which the outcome and impact of a training program may be determined. Reaction assesses the immediate effects on the participants as to their feelings toward the training. This offers an assessment of the participants' receptivity to the training, and can be an important factor in determining what is learned. Learning, the second stage, looks at the information—principles, facts, techniques—absorbed by the trainees. While learning is important in the training process, it must result in some job behavior as the next logical step in making the desired changes. It is in the final stage, results, that we can start to measure impact. Kirkpatrick describes this in terms similar to other evaluation researchers, who consider the objectives of the training as a guide to determining its impact. His examples describe measures such as cost reduction and reduced absenteeism as indicators of training program impact.

Why Do Impact Evaluation?

Impact evaluation is a purposeful activity, undertaken to affect policy and institutional development, to shape the design and implementation of future interventions, and to improve the management of training and development programs. Impact evaluations can

- Provide a measure of institutional, economic, social, and political change that has resulted from training and institutional development interventions by identifying the extent to which these interventions have helped to solve the problems they set out to address; the observable effects on individual, institutional, and sectoral performance and/or on policies; and the changes in the population's quality of life.

- Increase understanding of the positive and negative factors that have contributed to impact, for example, conditions in the environment, appropriateness and effectiveness of intervention strategies.

- Provide a basis for decisionmaking about future action based on analysis and discussion of the findings.

A donor agency or a training and research institution may have a number of reasons for undertaking impact evaluations, including the following:

- *Maintaining accountability.* Impact evaluation maintains accountability by following the use of public funds through to the organization's ultimate goals.

- *Completing the training cycle and keeping in touch with the client base.* In a certain sense, impact evaluations are the last chapter in the history of an activity or program that began some years earlier with the writing of the objectives and the design of the activity.

- *Providing a source of lessons to guide future action.* Going beyond the accountability requirements, training institutions and donor agencies have discovered the benefits of going to the beneficiaries to find out what results they are getting from their interventions so as to learn from their experience and to guide future actions.

The African Development Bank carries out impact evaluations to identify the results of its activities, to feed into needs assessment for future programming, and to establish ongoing consultative mechanisms with beneficiaries. The bank uses focus groups where former participants influence the content of future programs based on their own experience of implementation (for more details, see appendix I, the Annotated Bibliography).

EDI's Infrastructure and Urban Development Division commissioned an impact evaluation of five years of activities in Sub-Saharan Africa and found that a number of factors increased the chances of impact on policy development: following up regional senior policy seminars with a national seminar, bringing together teams of key stakeholders from various ministries for regional seminars and representatives of all key institutions for national seminars, and so on. These and other lessons from the impact evaluation helped to shape future activities into consciously integrated strategies and programs.

The Instituto Interamericano de Cooperación para la Agricultura in Costa Rica has designed elaborate follow-up and evaluation mechanisms. These feed into decisionmaking structures that are participatory (including the lead and beneficiary institutions), and inform decisions on programming training on an ongoing basis. The evaluation process also helps develop all parties' institutional capacity to carry out continuous self-assessment (for details, please refer to the Annotated Bibliography).

Capacity-building programs funded by multiple donors in Africa built mid-stream assessments into their design so that they can adjust their activities for maximum impact in the longer term, for example, the Municipal Development Programme to strengthen institutional capacity in the municipal sector, and the Agricultural Management Training Programme.

What Have We Learnt from Impact Evaluations of Training Activities and Programs?

Evaluations have shown that a number of factors contribute to impact, namely:

- *Relevance* of knowledge, techniques, and skills to the job (when dealing with skills development), of policy issues to problems policymakers face (in policy development processes), and of institutional development activities to the short- and long-term capacity development needs of the institution.

- *Ownership* by the key stakeholder institutions in the countries of the activity or program, particularly in policy and institutional development projects and programs.

- *Commitment of participants to and support from the institution* for new initiatives undertaken in the context of the activity. This is closely linked to relevance and ownership.

- *A favorable policy and/or institutional development context* in the country.

- *Selection* of participants who represent appropriate institutions and are in a position to use the knowledge, apply the skills, and influence policy processes and management decisionmaking.

- *Continuity* of participants in the activity in the organization, that is, they should remain long enough to have an impact.

- *Material conditions* to implement what participants learn, that is, technology and equipment, materials, and funds.

- *A well-designed training activity that responds to a clearly identified need, is part of an integrated programmatic strategy, is spread out over many years, and/or is designed to deal with an identified blockage in the policy or institutional development process.*

Impact evaluations have confirmed that much of the activity that EDI and its partner institutions are involved in feeds into complex policy and institutional processes where many factors intervene.

To what extent can one measure or observe changes that could be attributed to the training or institutional development activities? What does one look for? What are realistic and credible indicators of change leading to development? Assuming that one can identify indicators, to what extent is it possible to demonstrate the relationship between the results and a given training institution's input?

This manual is intended to assist trainers and managers of training institutions, as well as program sponsors and managers of development projects with little training in evaluation, who may be thinking about undertaking an impact evaluation of their activities or may be about to embark on such an evaluation. The manual will not make anyone a specialist in evaluation, for example, it

EDI and FASID wanted the impact evaluation to result in guidelines that staff could incorporate in future activities. The evaluation assessed the activities in relation to the program's objectives. The project analysis and management skills participants learned in these courses showed only a moderate short-term impact in the face of the objective stated earlier; however, the evaluation permitted trainers to clarify the program's long-term objectives, for which gains were found to be significant. The following are some of the characteristics of the activities and the related lessons from the impact evaluation:

- *None of the non-Japanese participants in the EDI-FASID program attended more than one course. The role that could be played by the continuity of participants through various courses and the concentration on specific countries to build up a critical mass of project planners and implementers in the countries, plus the role of follow-up activities in capitalizing programmatically on the EDI-FASID investments already made, came up as important untapped issues in the evaluation.*
- *Analysis showed that even though the activity objectives had been fulfilled, insufficient importance had been paid to overall program objectives in this series of linked activities. This pointed to the need to appoint an overall EDI coordinator for the entire program.*
- *The deficiency and conciseness of the training materials used for the seminars noted in the evaluation exposed the need for curriculum planning and development of course materials.*
- *The Japanese participants had been selected by the Japanese Civil Service, and, as a group, faced difficulties in the activities compared to participants from developing countries. The evaluation recommended having FASID participate actively in choosing Japanese candidates and holding simultaneous short courses for the Japanese participants in development economics and in spoken English during the activity so that they could make full use of future activities under this program.*

does not go into the technical details of sampling and statistical analysis. It does, however, seek to provide enough information on methodologies that undergird sound evaluation practice to help readers make reasonable methodological choices and sufficient details to allow readers to implement these choices.

2

A Collaborative Approach

Impact evaluation activities logically fall under the general rubric of "applied" research. The main rationale for doing applied research is to affect the actions and thinking of people who bring about development change and who may use the findings and conclusions evaluators provide to inform future decisions and actions.

Governing councils, senior management of lead or partner training institutions, or funding agencies are usually the initiators of a request to carry out impact evaluations. They may need the study for any number of reasons: accountability, as a basis for decisions on program continuation and future funding, as a source of institutional learning in critical areas of intervention, and so on. Training institutions that have not initiated the evaluation, but nevertheless have a stake in it, may be able to use the impact evaluation process and results as a source of lessons to improve their interventions in the future.

Stakeholders in Evaluation

Whatever the impetus, evaluators conduct their work in a real-world setting of multiple, and sometimes conflicting, interests. The ultimate beneficiaries of training and development interventions—the people whose quality of life is affected by policies and services provided by institutions in their countries—may have a stake in the results of the evaluation. In practice, however, stakeholder groups concerned with any given evaluation effort consist of those who have direct interests in the program. Interventions in training, policy, and institutional development focus on strengthening institutions as an intermediate step to improving people's quality of life.

So who are the parties typically involved in or affected by evaluations? Listed below are some of the stakeholder groups that may either directly participate in or become interested in the evaluation process and its results:

- *Policymakers and decisionmakers:* people responsible for deciding whether a program is to be instituted, continued, discontinued, expanded, or curtailed.

- *Program sponsors:* organizations that initiate and fund the program to be evaluated.

- *Program management:* the group responsible for overseeing and coordinating the training or institutional development program.

- *Program staff:* trainers, consultants, and researchers responsible for actual delivery of the intervention.

- *Target participants:* people and institutions who participate in the program or receive the training or institutional development interventions being evaluated.

- *Contextual stakeholders:* organizations, groups, and individuals in the environment of the program who have a stake in the results of the evaluation, for example, central and local government officials and community groups.

- *Evaluation manager:* the person or unit responsible for managing the evaluation process, including writing the terms of reference for the evaluator or evaluators, recruiting the evaluators, providing logistical support to the evaluation, and receiving the report on behalf of the initiators of the evaluation.

- *Evaluator(s):* groups or individuals responsible for the design and conduct of the evaluation.

Although the list does not include all the parties who could conceivably be involved in what Rossi and Freeman (1993) call the "politics of evaluation," it does represent the stakeholders who most often pay attention to an impact evaluation's outcomes and who may participate in it in one way or another.

Academics and managers continue to debate the relative merits of "objective" evaluations—evaluations carried out by outside observers who are presumably not "contaminated" by the various stakeholders—versus more collaborative evaluations that involve several stakeholders in the process. Managers who are most concerned with accountability and verification of compliance with the terms of a project or program have tended to prefer calling on outside observers to carry out the evaluation. Others, whose primary concern is understanding the dynamics of complex economic, political, or social processes and/or building commitment of key stakeholders to future decisions and action, are increasingly considering adopting a collaborative approach to impact evaluations, involving several stakeholders in the process.

Assumptions That Underlie a Collaborative Approach to Impact Evaluation

The approach proposed in this manual stems largely from the author's experience with impact evaluation of training and institutional development programs in developing countries, and is methodologically well supported in the literature. It also reflects some fundamental assumptions and beliefs that lie at the core of a collaborative approach, namely:

Assumption 1: It is possible to combine methodological rigor and collaborative/participatory approaches to impact evaluation so that the findings are valid and the evaluation report is credible. Maintaining a distance from the stakeholders to safeguard objectivity does not necessarily lead to less evaluation bias.

Assumption 2: Actively involving the key people who have a stake in an impact evaluation in shaping that evaluation helps to focus it on meaningful and appropriate issues and increases the relevance of the evaluation, the sense of ownership, and the likelihood that the results will be used.

Assumption 3: A collaborative impact evaluation approach can constitute a learning activity and build up institutional capacity for self-evaluation and self-development.

Assumption 4: Impact evaluation is a process whose development usually turns out to be iterative and reflects the objectives, context, and circumstances of individual activities and programs. It is primarily an investigative process, and the methodology must be tailored to the specifics of the situation. Nevertheless, general principles and techniques can be identified from which evaluators can select those relevant and appropriate to the particular situation.

The following chapters propose a practical, collaborative approach to impact evaluation that is methodologically well grounded, yet flexible enough that evaluators can adapt it to different situations, and whose aim is to produce useful information for decisionmakers and information users. It is based on the steps outlined in figure 2-1. Key questions, basic principles, and practical suggestions are identified at every stage. Specific examples, as well as the EDI-FASID case study, are provided for illustration. Because the design of an evaluation is critical, chapters 3 through 6 devote considerable attention to this aspect of collaborative impact evaluation.

Figure 2-1.   *Steps in the Collaborative Impact Evaluation Process*

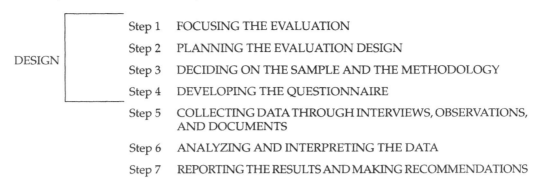

	Step 1	FOCUSING THE EVALUATION
	Step 2	PLANNING THE EVALUATION DESIGN
DESIGN	Step 3	DECIDING ON THE SAMPLE AND THE METHODOLOGY
	Step 4	DEVELOPING THE QUESTIONNAIRE
	Step 5	COLLECTING DATA THROUGH INTERVIEWS, OBSERVATIONS, AND DOCUMENTS
	Step 6	ANALYZING AND INTERPRETING THE DATA
	Step 7	REPORTING THE RESULTS AND MAKING RECOMMENDATIONS

3

Step 1: Focusing the Evaluation

The first step is to focus the evaluation to ensure that the evaluation issues are clearly formulated. This becomes the touchstone for each subsequent step in the evaluation.

Clarifying the Purpose of the Evaluation and Its Users

One major advantage of a collaborative approach to impact evaluation is that it allows different parties to specify the objectives of the evaluation. Because impact evaluation means different things to different people, and because different stakeholders may have different interests in an impact evaluation, gaining agreement from the outset on the purpose, expectations, and potential users of a particular evaluation is critical.

An important consequence of the existence of multiple stakeholders is that evaluators are often unsure whose perspective they should take into account when designing the impact evaluation. Is the proper perspective that of the participants, the ultimate beneficiaries, national governments, the managers of target institutions, the sponsoring agency, the program staff, or their own? The responsibility of evaluators is not to view one of the many perspectives as *the* legitimate one, but to be clear from which perspectives a particular impact evaluation is being undertaken, while explicitly recognizing the existence of other perspectives.

If an evaluation is to be useful, the users of the findings must perceive it to be relevant to the problems and issues they face at the time the evaluation is undertaken. Once evaluators have identified potential users of the study, consulting them directly is often helpful, as is consulting the proceedings of decisionmaking bodies, for example, steering committees, boards, or management committees, to get a sense of the issues and problems they face and of the decisions they may have to make in relation to this or similar programs in the future.

In 1993, both EDI and FASID wanted a comprehensive assessment and synthesis of the lessons from planning and managing both the program as a whole and the six individual courses. The terms of reference for the external evaluators identified for them the intended audience and the purpose of the evaluation. The choice of the external evaluators—one came from a Japanese research institute and the second from an American university—reflected the nature of the work.

EDI and FASID agreed that the review of the program and of the individual courses should consist of the following:
- *The program's objectives and validation;*
- *The program's coherence;*
- *The courses' objectives, approaches to these objectives, and identification of beneficiaries;*
- *The instructional design of the activities; their cognitive, psychological, and social aspects; and the location of the learning activities;*
- *The impact of the activities and lessons learnt;*
- *The follow-up activities for sustaining and disseminating the program's benefits.*
  The evaluation would also assess
- *The division of labor between FASID and EDI*
- *The cost-effectiveness of the six courses.*

Identifying Who Needs to Be Involved, When, and How

While including all the stakeholders in an impact evaluation team or consultative group is neither practical nor desirable, involving relevant and interested decisionmakers, information users, and stakeholders in a formal or informal way from the beginning develops ownership and commitment.

The division chief of EDI's former Infrastructure and Urban Development Division included his staff throughout the whole impact evaluation process. They participated in the initial meetings to clarify the goals of the evaluation with the evaluators, offered critical suggestions for improving the clarity and relevance of questionnaires, and participated in debriefing sessions to analyze the evaluation's findings and formulate practical recommendations for improvement.

EDI and the Centre on Integrated Rural Development for Asia and the Pacific undertook an impact evaluation of their joint program. A team consisting of one training manager from EDI, one from the center, and an independent evaluator agreed on the purpose and objectives of the evaluation, designed and carried out interviews, analyzed the findings, and made joint recommendations to the two institutions.

Where a team approach is not feasible or appropriate, ensuring that both the main users of the evaluation and the evaluators have agreed on the intended audience for the report and on the purpose of the evaluation is vital. Involving those stakeholders whose support will be needed to implement the various steps of the evaluation process can help to develop ownership of the process and greater commitment to follow through on recommendations.

EDI asked the China Network for Training and Research on Health Economics and Finance to participate in the impact evaluation of the first three years of the network's activities. The network's coordinator helped define the indicators of impact; reviewed the methodology, content, and translation of the questionnaires; provided logistical support for mailing questionnaires; and commented on the draft of the evaluation report. The preliminary findings of the evaluation, which were presented to the network's members, led to early commitment to act on issues that it identified, thereby paving the way for adoption of the report's recommendations.

Reviewing Objectives, Strategies, and Intended Impacts of the Program or the Activities

It is axiomatic in training and development, in planning, and in management that if you do not know where you want to go, then you will have great difficulty in figuring out how to get there. You also will not know if or when you have arrived. Training goals and statements of objectives are extremely helpful in focusing training programs and activities and are useful to go back to when doing an impact evaluation. The flip side is, of course, that if you do not know where you are going, you will never get lost, which is probably why so many training programs do not have training objectives!

The notion that change in an institution, a sector, or a nation can be observed and measured by an impact evaluation presupposes that training and development interventions proceed from a theory of action (figure 3-1).

Action is presumably triggered by a need. The need may be to develop individuals' specific knowledge and skills or institutional capacity or to resolve certain social and economic problems.

Figure 3-1. A Theory of Action

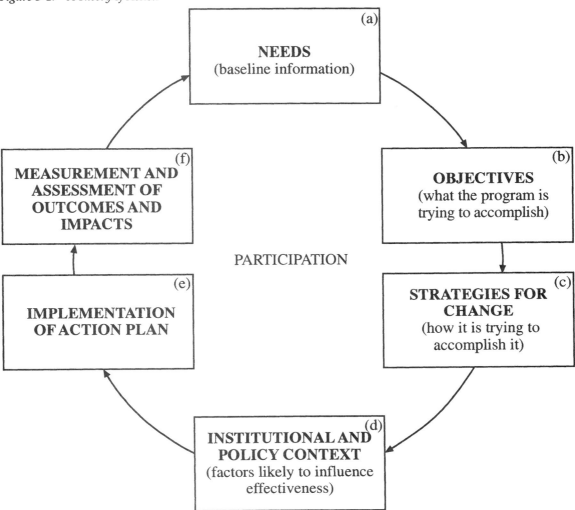

The theory of action basically states (a) what the needs to be addressed are; (b) what the activity or program hopes to do to meet the identified need, that is, its objectives; (c) what strategy of intervention is adopted to meet the objectives, or in other words, the strategies for change; (d) what assumptions are made about the factors that are likely to influence whether the desired change happens; (e) how implementation will be carried out, or the means to operationalize the change strategy; and (f) how measurement and assessment of outcomes and impacts will take place.

The theory of action guiding training and development interventions is rarely stated explicitly. A good place to start reconstructing the implicit theory of action is to review all the documentation about the intervention, such as training needs identification, institutional and policy assessments, activity or program initiating and monitoring documents, activity summaries and end-of-activity evaluations, agreements, and terms of reference written up between partner institutions.

Some activities or programs are developed in a systematic fashion with well-documented analysis and design. For example, training and institutional development programs funded by international donor agencies sometimes require the use of a logical framework analysis to plan the activity or program. Logical framework analyses link objectives to the factors in the institutional, social, and political context that are likely to influence effectiveness and to expected outcomes and impacts.

> *Consider the objectives and expected outcome statements of the EDI-FASID joint training program on social sector investment:*
>
> *"The overall objective of the program is to demonstrate the high return of investment in the social sectors, with a view to increase the share of resources channeled into these sectors in selected developing Asian countries . . .*
>
> *Expected outcomes are*
> - *A higher priority for the human resource development sectors in the countries invited, to be reflected in a larger and more cost-effective allocation of resources to the sectors.*
> - *An improved capacity for dialogue between the World Bank and Japanese aid agencies and the countries, as well as within the central and the sectoral ministries of each participating country."*

This is a useful starting point. (In addition to logical framework analysis, other approaches to modeling the projected results of projects and programs are systems analysis, causal networks, process modeling, and path analysis. See Valadez and Bamberger 1994, pp. 75–109.)

Even if the document review does not provide all the answers, an examination of the documentation will usually provide some leads on where to start looking for impacts.

The program's objective is stated in terms of what the program's designers intend to do, for example, demonstrate that investment in the social sector can bring high returns. The anticipated change in participants' outlook, that is, participants will consider reviewing their budgetary allocations to the human resource development sector as a result of the activity, could be inferred from the statement above and validated with program staff. Interviews with individuals involved in planning the activity and commissioning the evaluation might be necessary to clarify the precise intent of the institutional development objectives and the expected short-term outcomes and longer-term impacts.

When the training institution's goals include organizational learning and capacity building, evaluators should make every effort to consult the key stakeholders about impact indicators. This is because even where consensus on the objectives exists, those who designed the program, those who funded it, partner institutions, decisionmakers, and other individuals and institutions may have different views about what would constitute valid indicators of program effectiveness and impact. A collaborative approach allows these different perceptions to surface, be analyzed, and be reconciled before data collection begins. Discussion of indicators often increases stakeholders' understanding of their own unstated assumptions about change and how it can happen, and can broaden the scope and richness of their predictions about likely impacts of their programs. Such discussions can also challenge them to be realistic about potential impacts.

> *A collaborative approach that permitted analyzing and reconciling the different perceptions had to be devised for the EDI-FASID assessment. The evaluators were to use all the documentation related to the program and the courses, as well as actual interviews with*
> - *Appropriate Japanese Ministry of Finance and World Bank officials*
> - *Relevant FASID and EDI staff*
> - *A sample of participants in Japan and other countries*
> - *Contributing resource persons in Japan and other countries.*
> *This would clarify the evaluators' assumptions and perceptions about the impact, thereby enhancing the credibility of the evaluation.*

In June 1990, specialists from nongovernmental organizations based in developing countries and from external agencies participated in a workshop in Geneva to develop indicators for evaluating water supply and sanitation programs. As with any participatory exercise, differences in perceptions led to a good deal of discussion. Impact indicators were mapped out at different levels (community, program, national, and global) and for different objectives (sustainability, effective use of water supply and sanitation systems, and replicability). These were subsequently enriched though field work. For details on the participatory evaluation approach to water and sanitation projects see Narayan (1993) and UNDP and World Bank Water and Sanitation Program (1990), both of which are described in the Annotated Bibliography.

Some documents identify the objectives and underlying change strategy. Consider the objectives and strategy of a regional senior policy seminar with national follow-up workshops:

> The objective of the senior seminar is to help former Soviet-bloc countries design more appropriate and effective social safety net schemes by enhancing the capability of the countries' officials to revise their social strategies by
>
> - Increasing the sensitivity of the Ministry of Finance to the critical importance of investment in human capital and the sensitivity of the ministries of Health, Labor, and Manpower to the importance of efficient resource allocation;
>
> - Exposing government officials to alternative options and concrete actions required to attain them.
>
> The purpose of national follow-up workshops will be to present to and discuss with a larger number of officials the major proposals emerging from the regional seminar, focusing on some of the issues more specifically relevant to that particular country.

Here, the objectives of the activities are spelled out, as is the underlying strategy for change: first convince the policymakers to consider investing in social safety net schemes and equip policy implementors with alternative options and strategies, then develop relevant strategies with more widespread ownership at the national level. Predictions of likely outcomes and impacts of such a program could be made in collaboration with relevant stakeholders, based on the objective statement and on their knowledge of institutional and national policy processes in participating countries. The impact evaluation would then validate the predictions and the effectiveness of the strategy adopted.

While reviewing the documentation does provide a good starting point, for the most part, evaluators will find objectives that are stated in general and vague terms, for example, "increasing awareness and understanding" or "strengthening the capacity of [an institution] in [a sector]." Such objectives are rarely supported by adequate baseline information and comprehensive needs assessments. Where expected outcomes are identified, they are usually stated in terms of activity outputs rather than of concrete, observable changes in the systems.

Under these conditions, the most helpful approach is to work with those who initiated, designed, and managed the activities and programs to reconstruct the objectives, strategies, and outcomes by asking questions about the change and the difference that was intended, for example:

- What actions and changes in performance would you expect from the individuals and institutions as a result of the activity or program?

- How would you expect these actions or changes in performance to make a difference in participants' work? In their institutions? In the sector? In the policy processes?

• What kinds of impacts could these changes have on the institutions? On the sector? On the ultimate beneficiaries?

By posing such questions, evaluators help program staff and stakeholders to (a) think through their assumptions about what outcomes and impacts they expect; (b) be realistic about the objectives and possible outcomes of their activities and programs; and (c) map out their change strategy or theory.

> *The stated objectives of the joint EDI-FASID program given before were very general. However, the evaluators identified more precise objectives, listed below, that they could study through observable changes in the system. The program was meant to enable*
> • *Japanese civil servants to interact productively with colleagues from developing countries;*
> • *Officials and private sector personnel from developing countries to understand Japan's development experience;*
> • *Japanese specialists to teach international audiences;*
> • *FASID to develop the expertise to deliver training in international development on its own.*

A relatively simple framework to help map out assumed and observed linkages between training and institutional development activities and results at various levels—on individuals, institutions, end users, and socioeconomic development in the sector—as well as over time, expected outcomes, and anticipated impacts is presented in figure 3-2. One merit of this framework is that it helps stakeholders to focus on their assumptions about the reach of their activities, that is, how far down the line they assume their activities can be linked in a cause and effect relationship to the target groups where impacts are expected to be found and over what time frame. The definitions of outcomes and impacts may also help to focus and organize the different levels of indicators that are expected.

The definition of indicators helps to focus on answering the question: How will we know when the outcomes or impacts have been achieved? How can this be captured?

Indicators are defined as explicit and objectively verifiable measures of induced change or results.

A review of training and institutional development programs sponsored by development agencies reveals what are often totally unrealistic expectations of impact. They often expect two- or three-year programs, and even one-shot training activities, to change radically the policy or institutional context in a country or region and affect the quality of life of poor populations.

Because human, institutional, social, economic, and political development are complex, long-term processes, evaluations must (a) proceed from an assessment of the situation before or at the time of the intervention if at all possible, and (b) identify what indicators of change can realistically be expected to occur within a specified timeframe after the intervention.

Consider the following example, taken from the list of indicators for the mid-term evaluation (after eighteen months of operation) of the Municipal Development Program for Sub-Saharan Africa, an institutional development program:

> *"Objective*
>
> *Build analytical and institutional capacity in Participating Local Government Institutions (PIs) in Africa.*
>
> *Intended Outcome*
>
> *African institutions involved in local government will have increased their capacity to develop their own ideas, set their own priorities, and manage their own resources.*
>
> *Indicator(s)*
> • *Numbers of strategic and institutional development plans developed by staff of the institutions*
> • *Plans developed in consultation with their constituency (where this used to be done almost entirely by Western consultants)*
> • *Financial and political support for implementation of those plans."*

Figure 3-2. A Framework for Mapping Out Assumptions about Impact

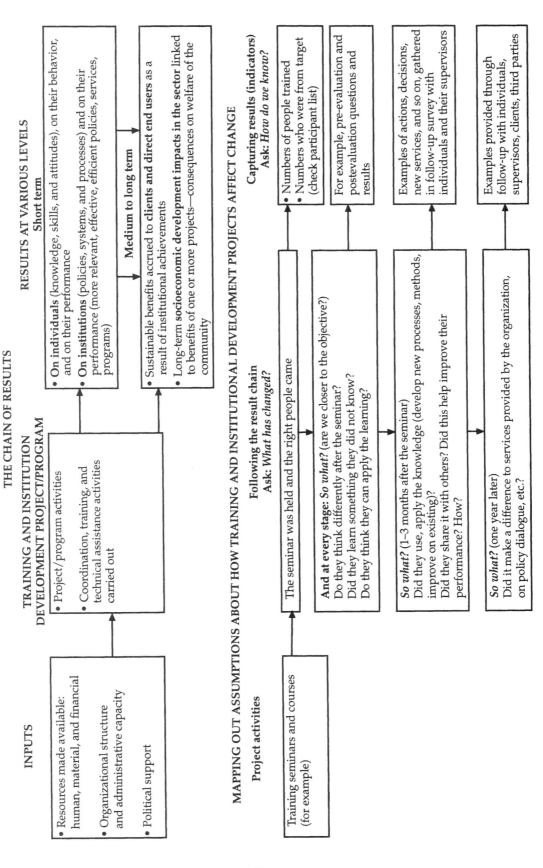

THE CHAIN OF RESULTS

| INPUTS | TRAINING AND INSTITUTION DEVELOPMENT PROJECT/PROGRAM | RESULTS AT VARIOUS LEVELS |

RESULTS AT VARIOUS LEVELS

Short term

- **On individuals** (knowledge, skills, and attitudes), on their behavior, and on their performance
- **On institutions** (policies, systems, and processes) and on their performance (more relevant, effective, efficient policies, services, programs)

Medium to long term

- Sustainable benefits accrued to **clients and direct end users** as a result of institutional achievements
- Long-term **socioeconomic development impacts in the sector** linked to benefits of one or more projects—consequences on welfare of the community

TRAINING AND INSTITUTION DEVELOPMENT PROJECT/PROGRAM

- Project/program activities
- Coordination, training, and technical assistance activities carried out

INPUTS

- Resources made available: human, material, and financial
- Organizational structure and administrative capacity
- Political support

MAPPING OUT ASSUMPTIONS ABOUT HOW TRAINING AND INSTITUTIONAL DEVELOPMENT PROJECTS AFFECT CHANGE

Capturing results (indicators)
Ask: *How do we know?*

- Numbers of people trained
- Numbers who were from target (check participant list)

For example, pre-evaluation and postevaluation questions and results

Examples of actions, decisions, new services, and so on, gathered in follow-up survey with individuals and their supervisors

Examples provided through follow-up with individuals, supervisors, clients, third parties

Following the result chain
Ask: *What has changed?*

The seminar was held and the right people came

And at every stage: *So what?* (are we closer to the objective?)
Do they think differently after the seminar?
Did they learn something they did not know?
Do they think they can apply the learning?

So what? (1–3 months after the seminar)
Did they use, apply the knowledge (develop new processes, methods, improve on existing)?
Did they share it with others? Did this help improve their performance? How?

So what? (one year later)
Did it make a difference to services provided by the organization, on policy dialogue, etc.?

Project activities

Training seminars and courses (for example)

17

Note that the statements are increasingly precise and observable as one moves from objectives, to intended outcomes, to indicators. The indicators in this example combine information that can be quantified (number of strategic and institutional development plans developed by African institutions) with observable, qualitative indicators of change: plans are expected to reflect local government constituencies, be developed by the institutions themselves, and be of sufficient quality to attract financial and political support.

The indicator statements above reflect the project team's assessment of the effects that they assume can be identified as far as possible down the cause and effect sequence to which their program contributes, and that can still be traced back to its interventions. They also reflect the changes that they assume can realistically occur in the eighteen-month timeframe, since the beginning of their program. While this sequence suggests a rather linear cause and effect relationship between objectives, activities, and results over time, the real world is far messier and more complex. Precise cause and effect relationships are unlikely to be easily traced.

While these indicators do not demonstrate an impact on the ultimate beneficiaries, their value is not diminished. Indeed, the attainment of the stated objectives as evidenced by measurement of the indicators may be of strategic importance to the program, because of its potential to create conditions for a longer-term impact on beneficiaries in the future, thereby creating impact leverage. This, of course, presupposes a theory of action that assumes that participatory development of plans can lead to improved performance by local government institutions, which in turn may lead to improvements in the quality of services to populations. For a more complete discussion of the notion of impact leverage, see USAID (1991), which is described in the Annotated Bibliography.

Whether the indicators are highly explicit or general, quantitative or qualitative, useful indicators are

- *Observable:* they state expected changes and differences in a way that can be recognized and described.

- *Credible:* stakeholders accept them as valid and reliable indicators of what they expected from the program.

- *Meaningful:* they are stated in language that decisionmakers and users can understand. Having rough measures of important objectives that stakeholders can relate to and make sense of may be preferable to having highly specific and quantitative measures of objectives that no one cares about or to which stakeholders cannot relate.

- *Realistic:* given the type of intervention, the complexity of the situation, and the time frame.

Lithwick's (1990) work has helped EDI evaluation teams to identify impact indicators for a number of the Institute's training programs. The approach proposed in this framework is simple (table 3-1). It starts from changes in knowledge, skills, and performance that can be observed in individual participants as a result of the intervention, proceeds through to consequences on institutions or on policy processes, and finally looks at impacts on society. Possible institutional development indicators might include those shown in box 3-1.

This section of the manual may appear to suggest that defining indicators is a systematic and logical progression from objectives to outcomes to indicators. However, experience with various groups of stakeholders has revealed that interesting and innovative predictions about change usually come from stories, anecdotes, and hunches from participating stakeholders. When encouraged to surface and be explored (rather than neglected because they do not fit into a logical analysis), they can generate new ideas to explore during data collection.

While indicators can help to focus the evaluation, the process must maintain enough flexibility to take the reality of complex change into account and to allow for the occurrence of unanticipated changes or impacts. The implication of this is that the methodology adopted must be both system-

Table 3-1. *Impact Indicators for Training in the Area of Policy*

Level	Examples of indicators
Individuals	Increased knowledge and skills, different way of approaching problems and policies, postseminar interaction (contacts and exchanges, promotions).
Individual performance	Application of skills, actions undertaken, adaptation of techniques and methods, problems solved.
Institution	Transfer of skills to colleagues and subordinates, changes in procedures, improved services (number, new and relevant, responsive tbeneficiaries' needs), improved financial management, increased credibility of the institution with beneficiaries, improved financial allocations to the institution.
Policy processes	Opening up of policy channels, securing of political commitment to change, increasing policy dialogue on alternative sectoral policies, setting up of interdepart-mental policy task force, increasing capacity to implement policies, mechanisms.
Policy outcomes	Effective decentralization of power to local authorities, budget shift from, for example, new road construction to maintenance (sector-specific).
Society	Improved services and quality of life for the beneficiaries, from intermediate institutions all the way to communities and populations (again, sector-specific).

Source: Lithwick (1990).

Box 3–1. *Institutional Development Indicators*

Institutional development indicators can include the following:
- *The institution's capacity to assess and forecast demand for its services*
  Indicators:
    - Consulting mechanisms
    - Communication links with funding sources, peer institutions, target groups, beneficiaries
    - Strategic plans
    - Correspondence between output of products and demand by beneficiaries
    - Methods of dissemination, marketing, and distribution
- *The institution's capacity for evaluating its performance and feeding back changes into the organization*
  Indicators:
    - Self-evaluation mechanisms and practices
    - Evidence of self-improvement as a result of evaluations
- *The adequacy and reliability of the institution's financial, human, and material resources*
  Indicators:
    - Staff size and qualifications
    - Policies to attract and retain staff
    - Budgetary resources and stability of sources
    - Infrastructure, equipment, and training materials
    - Strategies for increased financial self-sufficiency
- *The institution's capacity to develop training materials*
  Indicators:
    - Relevance and effectiveness of materials developed

The evaluators of the EDI-FASID courses were developing indicators for the entire program of activities. The impact of the courses was assessed indirectly through interviews and questionnaires on course satisfaction, use of acquired learning in job performance, effects of attending a course on job change or promotion, additional work-related skills and knowledge acquired, and the general perception of long-term relevance and usefulness of the course. Direct measurement of course effectiveness was not possible, because

- *No direct quantifiable measure had been developed before the activities;*
- *Given the multiple objectives of each course, a single quantitative or qualitative indicator of the effect of course participation would have been highly controversial;*
- *Even if some end-of-course measures of effectiveness existed, there were no baseline data to measure growth resulting from course participation.*

atic enough to check predictions and sufficiently open-ended to allow evaluators to find out how things really worked.

The example raises a number of practical difficulties in working with indicators. At one extreme, simply using the number of participants in a course is highly unsatisfactory—it says nothing about changes in behavior or in the workplace that might have occurred following the seminar. At the other extreme, a long list of indicators may be so comprehensive that only an extremely sophisticated computerized system could possibly track them.

There is no rule about how many indicators should be used to assess a program adequately. Program managers must use their judgment, and perhaps rely on some advice from evaluation experts to choose indicators that (a) will be seen as credible by key stakeholders of the program; (b) are the most important to track for learning, future decisionmaking, and accountability purposes; and (c) are sufficient to cover adequately the program's central objectives, while not so numerous as to make data collection so time-consuming that it becomes impractical.

Finally, a lack of baseline data makes any judgment about impact suspect. Gathering baseline data to allow for preprogram and postprogram comparison is highly recommended. Evaluation specialists and other experts can do fairly sophisticated baselines studies, including institutional assessments. Where such expertise is not available, or where the cost is simply prohibitive, it is nevertheless important to gather even basic baseline information concerning the key indicators the program manager will want to evaluate as the program is designed. This is not only helpful for eventual impact evaluation, it is simply good design practice. If such a baseline study has not been done, evaluators may use the impact evaluation exercise to provide such a baseline for future programs.

4

Step 2: Planning the Evaluation Design

Just like any other training and development activity, an impact evaluation has to be planned, organized, and monitored. The person managing the evaluation will have a number of responsibilities, namely:

- Preparing the initiating memorandum, clarifying the purpose and objectives of the impact evaluation, and making decisions on timing;

- Deciding on the members of the team if a team approach is to be used;

- Determining which team members are responsible for what parts of the evaluation and the relationship between the manager of the evaluation and the evaluator(s);

- Writing the terms of reference for consultants and getting agreement on methodology and the schedule for completing activities;

- Recruiting the consultants, including the search, selection, and contracting procedures;

- Preparing background documentation;

- Maintaining the focus of the evaluation, ensuring the appropriateness and credibility of the methodology, and supervising the study's progress;

- Facilitating logistics for data collection, which may include mailing and receiving questionnaires, making travel and accommodation arrangements, and setting up facilitating arrangements for interviews with former participants and stakeholders;

- Liaising with the evaluators on matters concerning draft and final reports;

- Communicating the findings to decisionmakers.

This section of the manual does not review all the activities listed, but covers the critical decisions that need to be made at the design stage of the evaluation.

The Decision on Timing

Impact evaluations of development projects are typically carried out several years after project completion. While adopting the same yardstick to decide on the timing of impact evaluations of training activities may be tempting, it may not always be appropriate. Experience with impact evaluations has shown that after four or five years, participants may have difficulty remembering specific training activities and their contributions. Often participants will have attended a number of courses given by various national or regional training institutions and donors, and attributing impact to a given intervention becomes increasingly difficult as other variables, such as changes in the institutional context, come into play.

If the evaluation deals with skills development activities (the short-term outcomes), it could be done as soon as three to six months after the activity. If the evaluation is assessing the impact of activities or programs on policy or institutional development processes, any time longer than eighteen months may make it difficult to separate out the effects of the training program from other intervening factors. In the end, the decision on timing will depend on an analysis of the process and what could reasonably be expected in a given period of time.

Thus the criteria for appropriate timing of an impact evaluation are that it is initiated long enough after the program has been in effect to measure outcomes and perhaps impacts. There should be a clear focus on which outcomes and impacts are being evaluated. Finally, the evaluation should be conducted when decisionmakers need such information and it can help them understand and identify alternative courses of action.

Internal versus External Evaluation

In the past, experienced evaluators and managers would go so far as to state categorically that evaluations should never be undertaken within the organization responsible for administering a project, but should always be conducted by an outside group. One reason outsider evaluations may have seemed preferable is that differences existed in the levels of training and presumed competence of insider and outsider evaluation staff.

The current evidence about whether inside or outside evaluations are more likely to be of higher quality is far from clear. However, a decision to bring in an outside expert is appropriate when outside content or evaluation expertise is required to give legitimacy to the findings and recommendations and when the use of qualitative or quantitative methodologies requires more knowledge of and skills in data collection and analysis than is available internally.

One common mechanism is to have in place advisory groups of one or more consultants to oversee the evaluation. The way such advisory groups work depends partly on the sophistication of the evaluators and the program staff. For example, major foundations often have advisory groups that meet regularly and assess the quality, quantity, and direction of the work. Some public and private training institutions with small evaluation units employ consultants to provide technical advice to the evaluators, to advise managers on the appropriateness of the evaluation unit's activities, or both.

A high quality, credible, and rigorous impact evaluation study may require a combination of different types of expertise: sectoral content expertise; expertise in evaluation design, data collection, and analysis; experience with policy or institutional development processes; and country or regional experience. In addition to such expertise, evaluators involved in impact evaluations of training and institutional development activities or programs should have the following qualities:

- Excellent communication skills, including interviewing skills, sensitivity to other peoples' contexts, and the ability to listen. These are essential as most of the data will probably come from interviews.

- Knowledge of institutional, policy, or development change processes, which is helpful in knowing what questions to ask and interpreting the answers.

- An understanding of the capacities and limitations of training as an instrument of policy and institutional development and the ability to ascertain the effects of other institutional factors on the impact.

Rarely will a single individual fulfill all these requirements, and the search for such a person often leads to dead ends, wasted time, and a great deal of frustration. This again points to the advantage of considering the impact evaluation as a team effort that brings together a number of people who together possess all the required qualifications. An assessment of the relevant knowledge and skills of internal human resources who could be part of an evaluation team can lead to realistic and optimum management choices for the composition of an evaluation team, including the recruitment of external consultants.

With multiple stakeholders, as in the EDI-FASID case, the evaluation process is almost as important as the findings themselves. If the evaluation is designed and carried out as a joint exercise, the various parties may ultimately develop more ownership of its findings, and consequently be more committed to acting on recommendations. In the impact evaluation of the joint program, EDI and FASID each nominated one external expert to carry out the evaluation jointly. EDI staff drafted their terms of reference, work program, a timetable, and objectives for the evaluation, because EDI staff had more experience with such matters, and FASID staff reviewed the proposals. The terms of reference also included a description of the qualifications the evaluators should possess and a breakdown of the funds required. The modified draft of the document, shown in appendix II, is an excellent example of a plan for an impact evaluation.

The staff of EDI's former Infrastructure and Urban Development Division wanted to do an impact evaluation of their training and institutional development activities in Sub-Saharan Africa. They hired two consultants, one with policy and evaluation expertise, the other with training and institutional development expertise, evaluation expertise, and experience in Africa. Sectoral expertise was provided by the division chief and task managers who accompanied one of the consultants throughout the field portion of the study. The task managers helped the evaluator by participating in debriefing meetings to discuss the outcomes of clusters of interviews. These discussions played an important role in analyzing the data and in exploring recommendations for future action.

The staff of EDI's Environment and Natural Resources Division considered a team approach to be useful for assessing the institutional development of partner institutions. The team consisted of one member from each of the institutions and one outside consultant with good interviewing and evaluation skills, willing to work with multidisciplinary teams and experience in doing so, and some content expertise.

When an organization decides to recruit an external evaluation consultant, a useful approach is to write terms of reference, which can brief consultants on what the impact evaluation is expected to accomplish. The terms of reference will also serve as a reference point for the manager, the evaluation consultant, and the team throughout the process. Terms of reference can include the following headings:

- Background to the activity or program

- Reasons for the evaluation

- Issues to be covered or intended outcomes and indicators to be evaluated (where they have been developed)

- Clients of the evaluation, including a description of lines of responsibility and ultimate users of the evaluation

- The evaluation approach, including the general approach, expected activities, available documentation, and so on

- Statement of qualifications for the consultant, including required academic background, substantive knowledge, and experience in evaluation

- Timetable.

Where a number of stakeholders who are in different locations have requested the evaluation or will find it of interest, circulating a draft of the terms of reference to them can be useful, because it can focus the evaluation and raise some issues that can be resolved before the consultant is recruited.

The Programme Unit of the Municipal Development Program in Harare, at the request of its steering committee, developed an evaluation framework and terms of reference for the mid-term impact evaluation of the program. These were circulated to the executing agency and to members of the steering committee for comments prior to finalization. Members of the steering committee asked that the terms of reference clearly specify that the evaluator was to be accountable to the steering committee as the client of the evaluation, and commented on the management of the evaluation and on the indicators. The modified draft terms of reference (see appendix III) were used in initial discussions with the evaluator selected for the job and were finalized with the evaluator's input.

The Benefits of Holding a Planning Workshop

If the evaluation is a complex and expensive exercise, it is worth considering a planning workshop, which can focus the evaluation and plan for it. If those involved in the evaluation can interact in person, this is likely to be much more productive than trying to arrange the evaluation by mail and telephone. In addition, a planning workshop can build ownership of the evaluation exercise from the start and may mobilize some support for its implementation.

A planning workshop can be facilitated by the evaluators, and its outcomes can include the following:

- A statement of the evaluation's purpose and clients. The statement includes a justification (why are we doing this evaluation?) and ends with the objectives of the evaluation study (how do we expect the findings to be used? in support for what actions or strategic decisionmaking?).

- A statement of the perspective that will be adopted.

- A statement of the methodology that will be employed, including specifics of the following:

  - Sampling

  - Instrumentation

  - Data analysis and procedures.

- The time schedule. Ordinarily, milestone events can be identified and used as monitoring checkpoints to ensure that the study is on track.

- A designation of roles and responsibilities.

- A budget projection, that is, estimates of resources (time, people, funds) needed to carry out the specified tasks.

- A statement of the expected end product.

Designing the Evaluation

The key to drawing sound conclusions from evaluations lies in study design. Establishing that a particular program or project led to the observed outcomes or impacts is difficult because three conditions must first be satisfied if causality is to be established. First, the evaluation must establish the temporal precedence of the "cause," thus for a training program the study would have to show that the training occurred before the outcomes or impacts. Put another way, the effects cannot take place before the proposed cause. Second, a measured covariation, or association, between the program and the outcomes or impacts must be apparent. In an ideal case, the effects of a training program—say, a change in how program participants make management decisions—would be observable among all the participants, but would not occur among similar individuals who did not get the training. Third, the observed association between the program and the outcomes or impacts must be nonspurious, that is, all competing explanations for the association should be eliminated to isolate the program as the causal factor.

Designs have been developed that address these three criteria to varying degrees. (For a thorough discussion of all the material in this section, see Valadez and Bamberger 1994, pp. 227–90.) The strongest such design is the randomized control group experiment. In this design, study subjects are randomly assigned to two groups. One group (the experimental group) participates in the program, and the other (the control group) does not. Evaluators measure the key outcome or impact variables for both groups before the program takes place, and then again afterwards. This design meets all three of the criteria as follows: (a) the evaluators can compare the behavior of the experimental group after participation in the program to the situation before the program, thereby establishing temporal precedence; (b) the evaluators can compare the change in the experimental group to any change in the control group to test for association between the program and the observed change among the participants and can use this comparison to estimate the size of the effect, if any; and (c) the evaluators should not observe any systematic differences between the groups—other than the program itself—that could explain any effects they see because of the random assignment of subjects between the experimental and the control groups. A number of evaluations employing this design have been carried out in bank work. Newman, Rawlings, and Gertler (1994) report on seven such evaluations in the social sector.

In most instances, however, a randomized control group design is impractical. For example, deciding randomly who shall and who shall not participate in a given training program is usually impossible, because participants either select themselves or are chosen by their sponsoring organizations. However, investigators have developed a number of alternative designs that mimic key features of the standard control group design. These are called quasi-experimental designs (see Cook and Campbell 1979). One variant uses the same basic design as the randomized control group design, except that the experimental and control groups are not randomly assigned. Unfortunately, this leaves open the possibility that some factor on which the two groups differ, other than participation in the program, might explain any apparent effects of the program. Evaluators can try several tactics to address this problem. For example, they could match the control and participant groups on variables that might reasonably explain any postprogram differences between them; however, this does not completely solve the problem. The very act of selection (or self-selection) to participate in a program ensures that the experimental and control groups are not the same.

This issue of selection is only one of a number of threats to the validity of any conclusions drawn on the cause and effect relationships between a program intervention, such as a training effort, and purported outcomes or impacts. These threats include the following:

- *History.* Before and after comparisons of program participants can reflect social, economic, or political events. For example, the death of an athlete from drugs during the time of a drug education program could influence attitudes toward drug use independent of the course materials. It would be easy to interpret the observed changes (or the lack of them) as program effects, even if no real effect has occurred. Control groups are designed to deal with this issue, but when assignment to groups is not random, evaluators cannot assume that the experimental and control groups actually experience the same history. One way to resolve this is by taking multiple measures of the key variables both before and after the program for the participants and the control group, which would allow evaluators to estimate any underlying historical trend, and thus help them isolate program effects.

- *Maturation or life cycle.* Learning styles, fatigue, boredom, or other internal processes unrelated to the program also may affect the outcome. As with history, these factors could result in apparent program effects where none exist or could hide real program effects. Again, multiple observations before and after the program intervention can help to identify these spurious trends.

- *Instrumentation.* Changes in the instrument used to measure outcome and impact variables can lead to erroneous conclusions about program effects. For example, the wording on a questionnaire or interview protocol might be different after the program than before or interviewers might have changed their technique. These changes could produce apparent effects that evaluators might erroneously attribute to the program.

- *Testing.* Sometimes participating in preprogram data collection (or testing), for example, by being interviewed, affects the postprogram responses of both experimental and control groups. Again, this could lead to incorrect conclusions about whether the program had any effect on the outcome and impact variables of interest. One way to deal with this is to have a second set of experimental and control subjects who are not subjected to preprogram data collection. This allows the evaluators to exclude the effects of the preprogram testing when analyzing data to estimate the program's effects.

- *Rivalry, compensatory equalization, and resentful demoralization.* These three threats refer to conditions that may affect the control group, thereby contaminating the results of the evaluation, and are especially important for training programs. Rivalry occurs when members of the control group respond to being left out of the program by trying harder, thus improving their performance on outcome and impact measures and reducing the measured effect of the program. By contrast, resentful demoralization among control group members is a deterioration in performance brought on because they know they were denied the treatment. The result is an exaggeration of differences between the control and experimental groups, and thus an overestimate of program effects. One way to deal with both rivalry and demoralization is to introduce a third group that is administered an innocuous program (a placebo) that should not affect comparisons with the experimental group, but will dispel the sense of being excluded. By comparing the control and placebo groups, evaluators can estimate the size of either rivalry or demoralization effects to get a better estimate of actual program effects. Compensatory equalization occurs when a decision is made (presumably by managers, not by evaluators) to provide the program to the control group anyway. This ensures that any comparison between the control group and the experimental group will not yield valid estimates of program effects.

Critics base their charges against quasi-experimental designs to deal with these and other threats to valid estimation of program effects on three grounds, namely: (a) the use of before and after data collection procedures means that these studies may take a long time to conduct; (b) the designs tend to be complex, often requiring considerable expertise in research design and analysis issues; and (c) the designs do not address fully the problem of nonrandom selection of participant and control groups, thereby leaving the conclusions in doubt.

Thus Valadez and Bamberger (1994) note the frequency with which evaluators use less robust (that is, weaker) designs in practice. One such less robust design involves before and after measurement of key variables on the participant group with no control group. The problem here is that all changes would be attributed to the program, even if other factors accounted for them. A second such design involves postprogram only measurement of an experimental and a control group. Evaluators would assume that any differences were a result of the program, even though they could not know if the groups were already different before the program was introduced. The third design uses before and after measures on the experimental group and after program only measures on a control group. This is somewhat stronger than the previous two designs, but without information on how much the control group changed during the period under study, valid estimates of program effects are difficult to obtain.

To compensate somewhat for these weaknesses, Valadez and Bamberger suggest several approaches. One is to try to get participants (and control groups if used) to reconstruct the situation prior to the program through recall. Such data can be unreliable, so Valadez and Bamberger recommend conducting independent checks where possible to ensure that the data are reliable. Such reliability checks can come from documents, interviews with independent sources of information, or re-interviews with participants to check the consistency of their answers. Despite the limitations, this approach could prove useful in evaluations of training programs. A second possibility is to use secondary data, such as records, surveys, and the like, to estimate conditions prior to the program. A third approach is to use multivariate data analysis techniques to control statistically for differences between participants and control group members. Fourth, Valadez and Bamberger note the utility of using multiple approaches or triangulation (see chapter 5). Finally, they point to the success of rapid appraisal methods as a way to bolster these less robust designs (see Kumar 1993 for a thorough discussion of this approach).

5

Step 3: Deciding on the Sample and the Methodology

Once the initiators of the evaluation have achieved clarity of purpose and determined who will participate, the next step is to begin considering specific impact evaluation design alternatives and strategies. Clarity of purpose helps in making decisions about the critical methodological tradeoffs in evaluation design, namely:

- Sampling strategy and size of sample: for example, representative sampling, case sampling, or other approaches.

- Approach: qualitative or quantitative?

- Data collection techniques: interviews, questionnaires, or other methods?

There are no prescriptions for the best methodological approach or data collection technique. The focus must be on selecting the methods that get the best possible data to answer adequately the primary decisionmakers' evaluation questions, given available resources and time. The emphasis is on appropriateness and credibility in addressing the key evaluation questions. The judgment on appropriateness and credibility involves considering the relative strengths and weaknesses of the approaches and techniques available for data collection.

Sampling becomes an issue in almost every impact evaluation, because we usually lack the resources to study more than a portion of the phenomena that might advance our knowledge. If decisions are to be based only on partial information, this information must be the most appropriate for answering the questions the evaluation poses.

All sampling is done with some purpose in mind. Evaluators and managers concerned with statistical significance and generalization of their findings to the entire population under study will opt for representative sampling, that is, defining a sample that is in some sense representative of the entire population. The term population identifies a group of people, agencies, places, or other units of interest that can, by definition, be placed together, for example, the population of local government policymakers from Sub-Saharan Africa, the population of training institutions that carry out research on health care financing in China, or the population of all participants that attended a particular training activity.

Evaluators and managers who are concerned about in-depth understanding of processes in their context will opt for sampling cases. If chosen appropriately and done well, case studies produce valid portrayals of change processes and impacts in their context, and thus provide a good basis for understanding the factors that contributed to success or failure. The problem with this approach is that the evaluators or other users of the findings may yield to the temptation of inappropriate generalization of case study findings to the entire population that was touched by a program.

A sample consists of a subset of elements from the population selected according to a sample design, which specifies the rules and operations by which the sample is to be chosen from the population.

Sampling Strategy for Quantitative Evaluations

Selecting and implementing a sample design requires evaluators to make many decisions. A wide variety of techniques for taking a sample is available, and which one is the best for any given study depends on a number of factors (see GAO 1992; Pedhazur and Pedhazur 1991; Valadez and Bamberger 1994). Three common methods are simple or systematic random sampling, stratified sampling, and cluster sampling (see table 5-1).

Simple random sampling is the basis of all statistically representative sampling methods. It is appropriate when the population to be sampled is relatively homogeneous and can be sampled from a single list. The most important feature of this approach is that each element of the population has precisely the same probability of being selected as a member of the study sample. A frequently used variant is systematic random sampling, in which only the first person is selected randomly, and then each nth person is sampled. For example, if we needed a sample of 100 students from a

Table 5-1.   *Representative Sampling Strategies*

Sampling strategy	Definition	Advantages and disadvantages
Random	Simple random samples are drawn by listing all the cases in the population to be studied, then a table of random numbers or a computerized random digit generator is used to select sample cases. A variant is systematic sampling. In this case a random process is used to select the first sample case from the population, then every nth case is selected until the desired sample size is reached.	Simple and convenient. May not represent all the desired characteristics of the population under study. A list of all members of the study population may not be available.
Stratified	The population is first divided into nonoverlapping subdivisions, called strata, based on one or more classification variables, which can include position, sex, size of organization, language group, or geographical location. The strata must be relevant to the key evaluation questions. Elements are then selected randomly within each stratum.	Can be used to ensure that sufficient numbers of cases within each stratum are sampled to permit separate group estimation. Can be costly and complex.
Cluster	Consists of sampling clusters, e.g., geographic area, training institutions, or all participants at a seminar. All elements of selected clusters are treated as the sample.	Practical, in that it uses easily obtainable lists, such as seminar, country. Economical, when geographic proximity of those sampled reduces administrative problems and financial costs, especially if interviews are required. The precision of estimates based on cluster sampling depends on the cluster.

Source: Adapted from Pedhazur and Pedhazur (1991).

population of 1,000, we could use a random number table to pick the first member of the sample from the list of all students, then take every tenth student until the sample reached 100.

Of course, populations are not always homogenous. Frequently, we might have reason to suspect that the impacts of a training program will differ for identifiable segments of the overall population. For example, if some participants in a training program are experienced managers, but others are less senior staff, we might expect the effects to differ for each group. In such cases we can use a stratified sample, in which the population is divided into two or more strata that differ on one or more characteristics. The keys are that each individual should fit unambiguously into one, and only one, stratum; that the strata should not overlap; and that the individuals in each stratum should be nearly alike on the reference characteristic(s). Then the individuals in each stratum can be randomly sampled. Stratified sampling is especially useful in situations in which simple random sampling would be unlikely to select enough members of particular subgroups to allow statistical analysis. In such instances, we could draw a disproportionately large sample from those subgroups, perform our analysis, then weight the findings for each subgroup to represent its actual proportion of the overall population.

Other instances may also arise in which using random samples may not be possible or convenient. For example, sometimes we might not be able to obtain a list of all the people in the population from which a sample is to be drawn; in other cases the population might be so widely dispersed geographically that the costs of collecting data (especially for in-person interviews) would be prohibitive. In such cases, cluster sampling may be an appropriate option. In this technique, clusters are randomly selected first, then all cases within the clusters—or a randomly drawn subset of such cases—are included in the study sample. In training programs, clusters frequently consist of particular sessions of a class or seminar. The major disadvantage of this approach is that it tends to produce less precise statistical estimates than the other methods discussed.

Of course, the characteristics used to define strata or clusters cannot be arrived at arbitrarily. Policy decisionmakers, program managers, and staff can help to identify appropriate variables that might affect the impact of training activities.

The program staff and division chief of EDI's Infrastructure and Urban Development Division thought that differences in impact in different countries might depend on whether the national policy and institutional context were favorable, and on whether participants attended in teams rather than as individuals. Thus, the sample needed not only to include participants, their supervisors, and so on, but also had to ensure that the countries selected offered a good balance of the identified variables, that is, countries with a favorable policy context and countries with an unfavorable policy context, countries whose participants had attended in teams and countries whose participants had attended as individuals. Given the different pedagogical approaches used in francophone and anglophone African countries, the division's staff also considered ensuring that countries from both groups were surveyed was also important.

Sampling Strategies for Case Evaluations

In studies where in-depth understanding of specific cases rather than statistical generalization is the goal, other sampling strategies are appropriate. Two broad approaches are available: convenience and purposive (for a fuller discussion see GAO 1990, pp. 22–30; Patton 1990, pp. 169–83).

Convenience sampling occurs when evaluators select cases merely because collecting data on them is easy. Often, evaluators do this type of sampling when particular cases are geographically accessible, as when the evaluators are already located in the countries, villages, or other units sampled. This approach is of limited utility, however, because the results tell us little beyond what happened in the particular cases examined.

- *Purposive sampling* involves selecting cases in such a way that evaluators can achieve the specific objectives of the evaluation. A number of such sampling strategies are available, including the following:

- *Bracketing or extreme case sampling* is used to obtain information about cases that are unusual along some important dimension, for example, the most and least expensive programs. The idea is that lessons on what happens under extreme conditions can provide useful information on what factors contribute to program success or failure, even under conditions that are more typical. However, findings based on extreme cases are vulnerable to being dismissed as unrepresentative.

- *Typical case sampling* can provide a qualitative profile of a program or those participating in it. Such data can be especially useful in communicating how the program works to those not familiar with it. Unlike data from extreme cases, those from typical cases cannot be dismissed as representing only the most unusual circumstances; however, the findings cannot be generalized to all circumstances either.

- *Maximum variation sampling* is a way to capture for evaluation a broad range of circumstances under which the program is being implemented. The idea is to capture any patterns that emerge across the range of conditions under which the program operates.

- *Critical case sampling* refers to a circumstance in which evaluators may be confident that if an outcome or impact occurs (or does not occur) in a particular case, it will (or will not) occur in others. This may take the form of the statement that "if it can succeed here, it can succeed anywhere." This approach can be useful where evaluators can only study one or a small number of cases, but it requires knowledge of what dimensions are critical to success or failure before cases can be selected.

- *Special interest sampling* occurs when evaluators select cases because they are especially sensitive or politically important. Often they use this approach when the client is particularly interested in one or more specific cases, or widespread interest in the cases is likely to attract attention to the study. The advantage here is that getting the attention of decisionmakers is more likely to lead to utilization of the evaluation's results.

One of the important things about purposive sampling is that each type requires evaluators to have some basic information on all the cases. For example, they cannot select a typical case unless they know how all the cases are distributed on the dimension of interest. Thus, purposive sampling is not a haphazard process, but one that requires a structured approach, with a clearly articulated rationale for the kind of sample selection employed and an appreciation for the questions that sampling can and cannot address.

Sample Size

Decisions on sampling strategy and size are complex, and are subject to a host of concerns, some technical, others organizational. The credibility of the findings will require that the sample include people who can speak authoritatively about what happened after the activities or programs and about both outcomes and impacts. These may include the participants themselves, their supervisors, their institutions' leadership, parent ministry representatives, clients and beneficiaries of the institutions, other institutions and agencies directly involved in the seminar or program (including decisionmakers and program staff), and others.

In the case of representative samples, the criteria invoked to determine when to stop sampling is a statistical confidence level that is deemed sufficient to generalize to the entire population and the technical requirements of the statistical procedure being used (see Valadez and Bamberger 1994, pp. 361–400). There are no rules for sample size when dealing with case sampling, because the criterion of validity and meaningfulness has more to do with the information richness of the cases selected and the observational and analytical capabilities of the evaluator, than with sample size. Sample size depends on what you want to know, the purpose of the inquiry, what is at stake, what will be useful, what will have credibility, and what can be done with the time and resources available. Decisions on sample strategy and size can often benefit from some expert advice. Interested readers are encouraged to refer to the many excellent books written on the subject (see the Annotated Bibliography).

Choosing the Approach: Quantitative and Qualitative Alternatives

Qualitative research is "a particular tradition in social science that fundamentally involves watching people in their own territory and interacting with them in their own language, and on their own terms" (Kirk and Miller 1986). Qualitative methods include in-depth, open-ended interviews; direct observation; the study of life and organizational histories; content analysis of written documents and certain archival, computer, and statistical manipulations.

Quantitative research originated in the natural sciences and involves measuring phenomena. Carmines and Zeller (1979) define measurement as a process of "linking abstract concepts to observable indicators," involving an "explicit and organized plan for classifying (and often quantifying) data in terms of the general questions in the researcher's mind." Quantitative methods are used extensively in survey research using standardized instruments and in cost-benefit analysis.

An extensive literature has developed around the use of quantitative versus qualitative methods in evaluation. The advocates of qualitative approaches stress the need for intimate knowledge of a program's concrete manifestations to attain valid information about its effects. In contrast, quantitatively oriented evaluators tend to be concerned primarily with cleanly measuring net impact. Often the polemics obscure the critical point, namely, that each approach can be useful, and that the choice of approaches depends on the evaluation questions.

In many ways, a tradeoff between qualitative methods and quantitative methods is a tradeoff between depth and breadth. Qualitative methods allow the study of selected issues, cases, or events in depth and in detail and the pursuit of unanticipated changes or impacts. Because data collection is not constrained by predetermined, standardized categories such as the response choices that constitute typical questionnaires, qualitative methods can capture the richness of people's experience in their own terms. Moreover, the understanding and meaning of events can be explored through the analysis of detailed descriptions and verbatim quotations. The tradeoff of using this approach is that it is expensive (time for data gathering, compilation, and analysis, as well as travel and field expenses) and may not lead to conclusions that can be readily generalized or replicated by others.

Quantitative methods, by contrast, permit statistical compilation (for example, of respondents' profiles and incidence of impact), analysis, and comparison of responses across large numbers of respondents at a much lower cost than qualitative approaches. Evaluators fit people's experiences and the variables that describe program outcomes into standardized categories to which numerical values are attached, thereby producing "hard" data that they can analyze statistically, either manually or using a computer. Moreover, the results should be amenable to testing through replication, at least in principle. The tradeoff of using quantitative methods is that they do not provide the depth of understanding qualitative methods can yield, and they do not allow the pursuit of unanticipated events. Also, because quantitative methods rely extensively on standardized questions, the quality of the data depends heavily on the quality of the questions, their clarity, and how respondents interpret them.

To illustrate the tradeoffs in the type of information the two different approaches provide, compare respondents' possible answers to (a) a standardized question on a questionnaire (quantitative), and (b) an open-ended question on the same issue (qualitative).

Standardized question:

Were national institutions and trainers sufficiently involved in designing and conducting the management training program?

	Not enough				*Sufficiently*		
a. Designing	1	2	3	4	5	6	*Average: 3.2*
b. Conducting	1	2	3	4	5	6	*Average: 4.5*

Twenty-two trainers responded to the question. On average, they were moderately satisfied with their involvement in designing the program and relatively more satisfied with their involvement in conducting it. Now, compare this result with one of the responses about the same issues using an open-ended question:

Open-ended question:

Please add any personal comments you would like to make in your own words about the program's approach to involvement of national training institutions:

I was looking forward to this opportunity to collaborate in design and delivery of this [sector] management training program. Most of the national institutions' trainers got to teach one segment of the course, although some of us got caught up in logistics. Our daily discussions to prepare, review, and adapt the modules helped to improve the way we were able to conduct them, but the organizers basically came up with the design of the program and we were asked for our comments. We have a great deal of experience in the region that the program could have benefited from, but given the lateness of our involvement, we could only make limited contributions.

Quantitative measures are succinct, easily aggregated for analysis, and easily presented. By contrast, qualitative responses are longer, more detailed, and help evaluators to understand issues from the participants' perspective and to identify issues to pursue further, but they take longer to analyze because their content is neither systematic nor standardized. Rossi and Freeman (1993) argue that qualitative approaches can play critical roles in monitoring programs and can add explanatory power to impact evaluations, and that quantitative approaches are much more appropriate in estimating the net impact, as well as the efficiency of programs intended to bring about institutional and social change. Other authors are not as prescriptive, saying that the choice of approach should be based on the type of data that will answer the evaluation questions and that will have credibility with the ultimate users of the evaluation (Rist 1989, 1994).

Experience has revealed that the use of multiple approaches and methods, often referred to as triangulation, can strengthen confidence in the findings of an evaluation study. Triangulation involves comparing results from three or more independent views of the data bearing on the same finding, for example, interviews with key informants, direct observation by the researcher, and written documents. This can be useful, because all methods are inherently biased in terms of the kinds of data collected, the sources of information, the level of analysis, and so on. Using multiple methods provides a way to offset the different biases of each method and to test whether the findings are sufficiently robust that they are not mere artifacts of any particular method (see Brewer and Hunter 1989 for an extended discussion of this point). However, using multiple approaches tends to be expensive and time-consuming, and so may not always be feasible.

Triangulation is an ideal approach, but it can also be expensive. An evaluation's limited budget, time frame, and political constraints will affect the amount of triangulation that is practical. Certainly, one important strategy for conducting evaluation research is to draw on different perspectives and to use multiple methods, and as already noted, one way to obtain a variety of perspectives is to use the team approach.

Deciding on Data Gathering Methods and Techniques

The following are the data gathering techniques most commonly used in evaluations:

- *Case studies* involve collecting information that results in the writing of a story. Definitions range from simple statements such as a "slice of life" or an "in-depth examination of an instance" to more formal statements like "intensive and complete examination of a facet, an issue, or perhaps the events of a geographic setting over time." Case studies can be descriptive or explanatory and serve to answer the questions "how" and "why."

- *Focus groups* involve holding a focused discussion with people who are in the population to be studied and are familiar with the pertinent issues before writing a draft of a structured set of questions. The purpose is to compare the reality about which respondents will be answering questions with the abstract concepts inherent in the evaluation's objectives.

- *Interviews* involve verbal interaction with one or more persons, where the interviewer asks questions, listens to respondents' answers, and records them. Interviews may be done face-to-face or by telephone, they may be formal or informal, and they may be close-ended (where the interviewer suggests a series of possible answers to specific questions) or open-ended (where the interviewer asks broad questions that can be followed up with more specific questions). Interviews are often supported by a plan of questions, known as an interview protocol.

- *Observation* involves observing and recording in a log or diary what goes on; who is involved; what happens, when, and where; and how events occur. Observation can be direct (the observer watches and records) or participatory (the observer becomes part of the setting for a period of time and observes processes, relationships among people and events, the organization of people and events, continuities over time, and patterns, as well as the immediate sociocultural contexts that may have some relevance or explanatory value).

- *Questionnaires* involve developing a set of survey questions whose answers can be coded consistently. Self-administered questionnaires are written and can be mailed or faxed. Questionnaires can also serve as an interview protocol for face-to-face or telephone interviews.

- *Written document analysis* involves reviewing documents such as records, administrative databases official reports, training materials, and correspondence.

Making the choice among the different data gathering techniques involves considering their appropriateness and relative strengths and weaknesses (see table 5-2).

Table 5-2.   *Data Gathering Techniques*

Technique	Strengths	Weaknesses
Case studies	• Can deal with a full variety of evidence from documents, interviews, observation • If well done, can add explanatory power when focusing on institutions, processes, programs, decisions, and events	• Good case studies are difficult to do • Require specialized research and writing skills to be rigorous • Findings cannot be generalized to total population • Time-consuming • Difficult to replicate
Focus groups	• Similar advantages to interviews • Particularly useful where participant interaction is desired • A useful way of identifying hierarchical influences	• Can be expensive and time-consuming • Must be sensitive to mixing of hierarchical levels • Not generalizable
Interviews	• People and institutions can explain their experiences in their own words and in their setting • Flexible–allow the interviewer to pursue unanticipated lines of inquiry and to probe into issues for depth of understanding • Particularly useful where language difficulties are anticipated • Greater likelihood of getting input from senior officials	• Time-consuming • Can be expensive • Sometimes the interviewer can unduly influence interviewees' response
Observation	• Provides descriptive information on context and observed changes	• Quality and usefulness of data highly depend on the observer's observational and writing skills • Findings can be open to interpretation • Does not easily apply within a short time frame to process change
Questionnaires	• Can reach a wide sample • Can be given to many people at distant sites, simultaneously • Allow respondents time to think before they answer • Can be answered anonymously • Impose uniformity by asking all respondents the same things • Make data compilation and comparison easier	• People are often better able to express themselves orally than in writing • Persuading people to complete and return questionnaires is sometimes difficult • The quality of responses is highly dependent on the clarity of questions • Often involves force-fitting institutional activities and people's experiences into predetermined categories
Written documents	• Can identify issues to investigate further and provide evidence of action, change, and impact to support respondents' perceptions • Can be inexpensive	• Can be time-consuming

Because of the relative strengths and weaknesses of each technique, a combination of techniques usually yields information that evaluators can cross-check, and the strengths of one approach can compensate for the weaknesses of another. In addition to strengthening the validity of the findings and offsetting biases inherent in various methods, triangulation has other advantages, namely: (a) the use of interviews before questionnaires can identify key issues that could then be subject to further investigation by means of the questionnaires; and (b) questionnaires can be used to support the findings of interviews, adding breadth and increasing the representativeness of the findings.

> *Staff of EDI's Environment and Natural Resources Division had conducted activities in more than twenty Sub-Saharan African countries. Time and budget constraints were such that they could survey only six countries through interviews. Having weighed the difficulties of obtaining responses from mailed questionnaires, they nevertheless decided that sending a short questionnaire to all former participants and institutions who could not be interviewed would broaden the sample at minimal cost and allow for broader comparison across the various countries.*

The choice of technique is a question of appropriateness, credibility, and available resources; however, whatever method evaluators choose, they must consult the end users. Note that an impact evaluation that relies solely on desk studies of in-house documentation may be the least costly, but it is also the least credible, unless it is followed up by direct consultation with the relevant stakeholders and intended beneficiaries.

> *The impact evaluation of the joint EDI-FASID program was based on a combination of document analysis, interviews, and questionnaires. The evaluators did not have the opportunity to observe any of the courses directly.*
>
> *The documents the evaluators studied included the terms of reference for the EDI-FASID collaboration and for each of the six courses conducted under the auspices of the program, the end-of-course evaluations, a follow-up tracer study for one course, and the completion reports for each seminar.*
>
> *The evaluators interviewed four officials—two from EDI and two from FASID—closely associated with the program and the courses prior to developing the questionnaire and again after the survey. The questionnaire dealt with the impact, preparation, design, content, administration, and follow-up of the courses using mostly questions with quantifiable responses on a scale of six. At the end of each section of the questionnaire, the evaluators asked participants for suggestions on how to improve the program.*
>
> *Evaluating the activities from the participants' point of view was particularly difficult because of the length of time that had elapsed after some of the courses and the geographical distribution of the 162 course graduates, who were spread across 26 countries. The participants' responses were gathered by means of 24 face-to-face interviews, 9 telephone interviews, and questionnaires faxed to 113 participants, for which the response rate was 45 percent.*
>
> *The choice of sample was based on feasibility and convenience, rather than on statistical methods. In such cases triangulation is all the more important to strengthen the validity of the findings. In the evaluation of the EDI-FASID program, "Interviews conducted with participants who also completed the questionnaire provided in-depth insight into their responses by allowing the interviewer to probe comments and criticisms. Interviews conducted with participants who did not complete the questionnaire extended the range of the information available to the evaluators."*

6

Step 4: Developing the Questionnaire

Evaluations frequently collect data through questionnaires that are mailed or used as a basis for interviews. However, no matter how elegant the technique used to formulate them, questions will yield useless data unless their content is meaningful. If the general approach to the impact evaluation is collaborative, the decisionmakers and information users with whom the evaluators are working are the major source of meaningful questions. Their involvement in the design of the evaluation and their intimate knowledge of activities and participants can help the evaluators focus on what information is needed and how the results will be used.

Another source of appropriate questions is a short period of field work in the program or institution prior to the larger survey. By reviewing documents, talking to former participants, learning their concerns and interests and even their specialized terminology (terms they use and understand), the evaluators can develop insights that will allow them to ground the questions in first-hand program experience. This is not always possible, especially when evaluating a program that was completed several years before, but it can be extremely helpful, especially if the main data collection instrument will be a written questionnaire.

A third source of questions is other mailed or interview questionnaires that have been validated in similar types of impact evaluations. Borrowing items from other instruments can be time saving and helpful when the evaluators want to make comparisons, but only insofar as the questions are appropriate and meaningful for the training or program being evaluated and the key evaluation questions.

Once all those involved have agreed on the basic content of the questions, it may be useful to have an expert evaluator work on the technical fine-tuning of the question items: refining the formulation of questions, developing scales if required, and so on. Pretesting questionnaires to get feedback from potential respondents is critical and can prevent costly data collection errors.

Five Essential Elements of a Good Questionnaire

Thoughtful, meaningful, and clear questions are the essence of any survey instrument. The technical knowledge and skills that evaluators typically acquire through their training and experience can add the essential clarity and precision to questionnaires. Individuals interested in developing their questionnaire design skills can consult some of the many social science methods and evaluation books dealing with the subject (some of which are reviewed in the Annotated Bibliography). Reviewing questionnaires with a skilled evaluator is also a good way to improve trainers' and decisionmakers' skills in formulating questions. The five main elements of good questionnaires are as follows:

1. *Keep the questionnaire relatively short and focused on the important questions.* Policymakers, managers, and sector officers have jobs to do and are unlikely to be enthusiastic about filling in a ten-page questionnaire with multiple sections, questions that repeat themselves, or requests for information that have little obvious bearing on the impact evaluation. Writing a concise and meaningful questionnaire is much more difficult than devising a longer, more elaborate one. Yet those who are being surveyed are more likely to complete a survey questionnaire if it is concise and to the point.

2. *Ensure that the instructions and the questions are clear.* Vague instructions can confuse and frustrate the respondents and produce information that is difficult to compile and analyze. Consider the following question taken from an impact evaluation questionnaire:

> *Please mark in order of priority the obstacles you have encountered when trying to apply the techniques and skills presented in the course:*
>
> a. *It was difficult for my colleagues to understand the techniques.*
> b. *The techniques/skills were not relevant to my job.*
> c. *My supervisors were not supportive enough.*
> d. *I did not have access to the necessary technologies/equipment.*
> e. *I realized I do not know enough to do something concrete.*
> f. *I needed more technical literature/support materials.*
> g. *I would have required other trained people who were not available.*
> h. *It was difficult to obtain necessary budgetary and manpower support to introduce the new techniques learned.*
> i. *It would have required too radical a change in the way we do things.*
> j. *There has really been no need to use the techniques so far.*
> k. *The bureaucratic constraints.*
> l. *I could not find enough funds.*
> m. *I needed data that were not available.*
> n. *The prevailing cultural/economic/political situations in my country do not allow me to apply the ideas discussed in the course.*

This question provides respondents with fourteen choices that they are to rank in order of priority. How the evaluator wishes that priority to be recorded is unclear. Should respondents circle their choices? Number them in order of priority? In addition, some of the choices deal with similar issues, for example, both (h) and (l) deal with funding constraints.

One way to get around a long question of this nature is to limit the choices to the five or six that seem most likely and to add a last choice called "other," with a request that respondents "please explain" or "provide details." The question could be reformulated as follows:

> *Did you encounter any obstacles in trying to apply the skills and techniques presented in the course when you returned to your work? Please check the box next to your answer.*
>
> ❑   *No*
>
> ❑   *Yes. Please identify the obstacles encountered in order of priority, writing a "1" next to the obstacle that was most important in preventing or limiting application of the technique/skill on the job, a "2" next to the second most important obstacle, and so on.*
>
> ❑   *The techniques/skills were not relevant to my job.*
>
> ❑   *My supervisors were not supportive enough.*
>
> ❑   *I did not have access to the necessary technology/equipment.*
>
> ❑   *The prevailing cultural/economic/political situation in my country does not allow me to apply the ideas discussed in the course.*
>
> ❑   *I could not find enough funds.*
>
> ❑   *Other. Please specify.*

While keeping the questions concise is highly desirable, going to the extreme of synthesizing several questions into one can also be confusing and frustrating for respondents, for example:

Did some factors <u>facilitate</u> or <u>prevent</u> the use of (training program) concepts and techniques by you and your colleagues after you completed training? Comment as you wish about <u>positive</u> and <u>negative</u> factors within and outside the project.

a) None interfered: ....

b) Within the project organization: ....

...

c) Outside the project organization ....

...

This question is really asking many questions within the same question. It also leaves little room to respond. If the evaluators consider information about positive and negative factors to be important, they should ask clearly about positive factors in one question and negative factors in another. They should also leave sufficient room for other useful information, for example:

What factors facilitated the use of the training program concepts and techniques on the project organization? ....

...

...

Please elaborate on any factors that may have facilitated the use of the concepts and techniques <u>outside</u> the project organization? ....

...

...

What factors prevented the use of the concepts and techniques on the project organization? Please give examples. ....

...

...

Training evaluation questionnaires often use rating scales. While they can be useful in recording quantifiable responses on questionnaires, evaluators should carefully assess their use, particularly where respondents may have difficulty in relating to the scales. Furthermore, the use of a rating scale does not preclude the need for clear questions and instructions. Consider the following question:

Were the follow-up visits by trainers <u>very useful</u> or <u>not useful</u> in conducting national team building workshops (circle number on the scale)

	<u>Not useful</u>				<u>Very useful</u>	
	1	2	3	4	5	6

Explain: ....

...

The first part of the question asks for an either/or choice, while the last part of the question requests that respondents circle a number on the scale. Assuming that many respondents would be familiar with the scale, the question may still yield valid data, but respondents could be influenced by the first part of the question and tend to respond at the extremes. The question could be rephrased to read as follows:

To what extent were follow-up visits useful in conducting national team building workshops? (Please circle the number that reflects your assessment most closely.)

Not useful at all   *Extremely useful*

1	2	3	4	5	6

Please explain the reasons for your rating ....

....

....

While it is possible to clarify and improve questions as an interview survey progresses, the mailed questionnaire offers no opportunity to clarify ambiguous questions. Pretesting draft questionnaires can feed improvements into the evaluation team's review process. Virtually everyone who has used questionnaires for data collection has a collection of anecdotes about misinterpretation. While they can be amusing, they can also have serious effects on the data collection process. Even a small trial run can be worthwhile. If the evaluation is large, as will often be the case in impact evaluation studies, the cost of not checking can be high.

> *The impact evaluation questionnaire faxed to participants in the EDI-FASID program consisted predominantly of simple questions with quantifiable responses on the impact, preparation, design, content, administration, and follow-up of the courses. The simplicity of the questions was crucial because of the diverse English language skills of the respondents, the lack of opportunities to explain any perceived ambiguities in the document to them, and their busy schedules. The questionnaire also solicited participants' suggestions on each of the topics to give them an opportunity to voice their opinion on any aspect of the courses. In the preparation of the questionnaire, the views of the course administrators (gathered from reports and during interviews) and the documents pertaining to the objectives of the program proved crucial. After the survey, interviews with some of the course co-directors and some of the participants who had answered the questionnaires gave the evaluators insights into the responses.*
>
> *As is common with mailed questionnaires, the initial response rate was poor. Even after aggressive, time-consuming efforts by EDI, FASID, and the evaluators to raise the response rate through telephoned reminders, collection of the Japanese responses by the FASID office, and so on, only 51 of the 113 questionnaires mailed had been returned by the cut-off date. Eight more arrived late and were not used.*

Evaluation team members coming from outside the national and institutional context in which the evaluation is being carried out, and who may also speak a different language from the one spoken by participants, face particular challenges. Questions formulated in one language and in a particular context may not be meaningful in another language or context. One advantage of working as a team is that complementary perspectives and knowledge (of substance, of evaluation process, and of context and language) can be mobilized to deal with these challenges.

Appendix IV contains an example of a questionnaire developed for an impact evaluation of a training and institutional development program in China. This questionnaire was first drafted in English by an evaluator with experience in evaluating training and institutional development programs who had lived in China for several years. An EDI sector expert who was fluent in both languages and two Chinese consultants reviewed the draft. Despite the technical accuracy of the translation, the questionnaire nevertheless had to be modified by the Chinese program coordinator in China to make it meaningful in the Chinese institutional context.

---

3. *Limit the questions to those needed for the evaluation.* Asking "interesting" questions that contribute little or nothing to the evaluation's findings runs the risk of reducing response rates and introducing unreliable information. Generally, evaluators should collect four types of data. First, *classification* information is used to assign the respondents to the correct groups: participant or control, pre- or postprogram interview. Second, *exposure* questions are used to measure whether and to what extent respondents received the program's services. Third, *outcome/impact* indicators measure the program's effects. Fourth, *intervening* variables are used to estimate the extent to which factors other than the program intervention (such as other programs, characteristics of participants and control groups) could have led to the apparent outcomes or impacts.

4. *Include a "no opinion" option for closed questions.* Closed questions force respondents to choose among the categories made available, but often respondents are not comfortable with any of the choices presented, and forcing a choice in these circumstances may result in the collection of unreliable data. Thus, giving respondents the choice of responding "no opinion" to questions about attitudes is important. Moreover, the presence of such an option legitimizes the notion that not having an opinion on a particular issue is acceptable, otherwise respondents often feel the need to express an opinion, even if they do not have one. One can make a similar case for including a "don't know" category for questions designed to test respondents' knowledge; however, not all survey researchers agree with this view. Some believe that forcing a choice is preferable, because otherwise many respondents will use the "no opinion" or "don't know" option to avoid revealing their views. The issue is particularly complex in the latter case, because the pattern of "incorrect" answers may carry policy implications.

5. *Use sound procedures to administer the questionnaire.* For in-person or telephone surveys interviewers must be selected carefully and trained properly. In addition, interviewers' age, sex, or other demographic characteristics could affect how respondents answer questions, for example, established professionals may be unwilling to provide sensitive answers to young student interviewers. In some cases interviewers may have to have specialized skills or knowledge, because of the technical issues addressed in the survey. Interviewers also need to be trained to ensure that the data they collect are reliable. This training should address a number of issues, namely:

   - The purpose of the study and the likely use of the findings;

   - The methods of selecting respondents (to the extent interviewers have discretion in this area);

   - The proper way to ask questions, record responses, handle nonresponses, and frame follow-up questions, where appropriate.

   Interviewers should practice among themselves during training, and those who actually go into the field should be selected based on their performance. Before the questionnaire is administered, it should be pretested. Pretesting can help determine whether the questionnaire is too long or too complicated and how willing respondents would be to provide answers. Moreover, pretesting can identify specific questions that are difficult for interviewers to ask or for respondents to answer, poorly worded questions, or other problems.

Finally, evaluators should have procedures in place to supervise the field work, for example, they might contact interviewees to ensure that the interviews were actually conducted, observe interviewers in the field, and review completed questionnaires promptly.

Sensitivity and Anonymity

While survey instruments are important sources of evaluation information, as a with most forms of data collection, they are also intrusions into people's lives. When designing questionnaires, evaluators should picture themselves on the receiving end of the survey.

Valid and useful responses depend on the respondents' good will. Explaining the purpose of the survey and what will be done with the information can help to create confidence.

If participants are guaranteed anonymity, the evaluators must honor this pledge.

Managers are acutely aware that the written word endures, and that what they say today could be used against them in ways unintended by the survey. By contrast, some may wish to be identified, especially if their opinions are subject to some supportive follow-up from the organization doing the impact evaluation. Nevertheless, unless respondents agree to be quoted, evaluators should guarantee that the results will be presented in an aggregate form that will not allow the opinions they express to be traced back to them. Obtaining permission from the client organization to make the evaluation report available to participants at their request may also help to generate trust and confidence.

Because background data on respondents is important for analyzing the data and detecting patterns, evaluators must obtain this background information in a way that does not permit identification of individual respondents. The first page of a questionnaire can be designed to elicit information on relevant background categories, such as the course attended, position, country, and so on (see the questionnaire in appendix IV).

7

Step 5: Collecting Data through Interviews, Observations, and Documents

Sample surveys are not the only way to collect evaluative data. Evaluators also use interviews, direct observation, and written documents or data files as sources of information. In general, having a structured instrument for collecting data from these sources is important to ensure that all field workers collect the relevant data in a uniform way.

Getting the Best Out of Interviews

In-depth interviews involve asking questions, listening to and recording the answers, and then following up with additional relevant questions. On the surface this appears to require no more than an articulate individual who can ask questions and listen. Experience has shown, however, that this is not enough. The purpose of interviewing is to find out what is in someone else's mind, to understand how they see things. This requires skill, sensitivity, concentration, interpersonal understanding, insight, mental acuity, and discipline in addition to the ability to talk and listen. In some cases, knowledge of the interviewee's culture is critical. Thus, interviewers should be carefully trained.

The assumption is that one can come to understand people's perceptions and constructions of reality by asking the right questions. The quality of the information obtained during interviews depends largely on the interviewer, whose job is to elicit responses from the interviewees while allowing them to use their own words to frame what they want to say. It is the interviewer's responsibility to provide a framework within which people can respond comfortably, accurately, and honestly to questions, while not influencing their responses.

Interviewing not only involves asking questions; it also involves establishing a rapport with those being interviewed. The initial contact is important in this respect. The interviewer must take the time to make introductions, explain what the evaluation is about, and clarify any points about which the interviewee may have questions.

> *In trying to obtain feedback on the joint EDI-FASID program from participants from twenty-five developing countries and Japan, the evaluators faced significant costs in terms of both time and money. One of the two evaluators who were interviewing participants was based in the United States and the other in Japan. To coordinate their work, allocate their time efficiently, and accommodate the busy schedules of some of the interviewees, an interview protocol was essential. The guiding questions for the interviews followed the stages of course selection and preparation, the content and delivery of the course and follow-up, and professional and social networking. This framework also reduced the problems arising from cultural differences among participants and between the two evaluators.*
>
> *Because of the length of time that had elapsed since some of the courses, which meant that the evaluators could contact only 113 of the 162 participants, and the budgetary constraints, the evaluators could only conduct face-to-face interviews with 24 participants from 4 countries. They also conducted nine telephone interviews with participants in five other countries.*

Participants may have forgotten details of the content and objectives of seminars or training programs whose impact evaluators are assessing. The evaluators may therefore want to start by stimulating the participants' memory by, for example, referring to the place where the seminar was held and people and events associated with the seminar. Skilled interviewers will ask open-ended questions encouraging the participants to recall the events as they remember them and to talk about what they want to talk about, confident that by the end of the interview they will have covered most of the relevant points.

Open-ended questions can take many forms. Learning how to formulate them so as to get people to express what they think and feel requires a good deal of skill. For example, simple questions such as those that follow could lead to an elaborate response on the part of a talkative person:

> *"We are really interested in finding out whether the training program is making any difference to participants in their work situation. Can you tell me about what happened after you returned to your job after the training? What were you actually able to do or apply?"*

These questions are open-ended and can get the respondents talking about the training: what they felt about it, what happened when they returned to their jobs, what actions they were able to take, what helped or hindered application of what they had learned on the job, what happened as a result of their actions, and so on. But interviewers may have to deal with shy or cautious people or with sensitive questions. In such cases they may need to provide some alternative examples to get the respondents talking, for example:

> *"We are really interested in finding out whether the training program is making any difference to participants in their work situation. Some participants have told us that they applied specific techniques to their work; others tried to convince their institution to consider their plan of action, with more or less success; yet others say they didn't really use or apply the knowledge or skills they were exposed to, but that they had started analyzing problems in a different way. Can you tell me about what use the training was to you, if any, when you returned to your job?"*

While alternative examples can be useful, interviewers should be careful of leading questions, that is, putting answers in people's mouths. Interviewers are sometimes too impatient to really listen. As a general rule, starting with a series of general, open-ended questions and listening carefully for clues, that is, words or phrases they can pick up on and pursue, is a good approach.

For an in-depth understanding of impacts and contributing factors, interviewers need to probe beyond generalities to get at facts, actions, results. They can do this by asking probing questions such as:

> *"You said [this] happened. Can you tell me more about it?"*
> *"Can you give me an example of, or show me [projects that you managed after the training program or new policies or procedures you adopted]? How are they different from how you did things before the program?"*
> *"What has changed as a result of the way you do things now [or the setting up of the new commission or department, or the adoption of the policy]?"*
> *"What was it about the program that contributed to the change?"*

After listening attentively to the answers, to ensure they have understood them correctly, interviewers may clarify or paraphrase by asking:

> *"What do you mean by . . .?"*
> *"Is what you mean [the following]?"*
> *"Am I correct in understanding that [what was understood]?"*

The manner and tone in which interviewers ask questions is important. Interviews are not interrogations. When people give up their time to participate in interviews, interviewers need to show genuine interest in their views and record them faithfully.

Interviewers should not be writing all the time during interviews, because doing so detracts from the conversation. If they can use a tape recorder, they need only take brief notes to highlight points of particular interest. Where they cannot use a tape recorder, perhaps at the interviewee's request or because one is simply not available, interviewers will need to take much more thorough and comprehensive notes. Writing down the main ideas, key facts, and examples during the interview can suffice if they have a good system of abbreviations, but they should complete the information right after the interview while the interview is still fresh in their minds.

Memory is fickle; depending on it can lead to loss or distortion of facts. The period immediately after an interview or period of observation is critical in terms of the rigor and validity of information. Evaluators should have at least half an hour after each interview or observation period to review their notes and fill in any blanks. This is also the time when they can jot down any additional information that would help establish a context for interpreting and making sense of the data.

The structured interview involves many of the same design and administration issues that apply to the sample survey. In addition to question wording, concerns arise about the order of questions; the need for pretesting and for expert review of the data collection instrument; and the selection, training, and supervision of interviewers. The discussion of these issues in chapter 6 generally applies here too (see GAO 1991c; Patton 1990, pp. 277–359).

Observation as a Source of Evaluative Information

Another way to gather data for an evaluation is through observation. Here, the evaluator directly observes, or even participates in, the program, and then reports on what happened. The advantages of this approach are that the evaluator can attain a better understanding of the program's context and is less reliant on preconceived ideas or on official pronouncements of how the program works. For example, Patton (1990, p. 202) reports that his own participation in a training program as part of planning an evaluation was critically important to understanding the program, which "bore little resemblance to our expectations, what people had told us, or the official program description."

Observation may take many forms. Patton identifies five dimensions along which such studies vary, namely:

- *The evaluator's role*. This refers to the extent to which the evaluator also participates in the activity under review. At one end of the continuum, as in Patton's example, direct participation can offer insights that no amount of more distant observation can provide. At the other end of the continuum, the evaluator is an onlooker, essentially outside the program. Where on the continuum a given evaluation falls will depend on "the degree of participation that will yield the most meaningful data about the program given the characteristics of the participants, the nature of staff-participant interactions, and the sociopolitical context of the program" (Patton 1990, p. 209).

- *The portrayal of that role to program staff and participants*. This can range from overt, in which case all staff and participants are made aware that the observations are being made, to covert, wherein they are not informed. There is always some concern that if participants know they are being studied, their behavior will be affected. Thus one argument for conducting covert studies is that they are more likely to reveal what is "really" going on, but this approach faces serious ethical objections. Normally, evaluations of EDI training programs would be overt.

- *The portrayal of the purposes of the evaluation.* Depending on circumstances, at times program staff or participants may not be fully informed of the purposes of the evaluation. For example, if the evaluator is worried that participants might be concerned that their performance—not the program's—was being evaluated, it might make sense to portray the study as something other than an evaluation. However, Patton argues that this can backfire, and generally favors full disclosure.

- *The duration of the observations.* The roots of observational studies lie in anthropology, where long-term immersion in a community or society may be important to achieving the desired level of understanding. Evaluation work generally requires much shorter time frames than anthropological observations.

- *The focus of the observations.* The evaluation might involve a broad effort to understand an entire program or be narrowly tailored to address a particular program component or concern. How broad the evaluation will be depends on the specific questions to be answered and the resources available to do the work.

As with surveys and interviews, having a formal instrument for collecting data from observations is useful. However, rather than a set of questions, an *observation guide* specifies the information that the evaluator will collect, such as the type and level of participation by participants in a training program. The evaluator can also use the guide to keep track of the frequency of certain activities, such as the number of times an instructor invites trainees to participate in group discussions. The more clearly the guide defines what is to be observed, the more useful it will be for subsequent data analysis (see Valadez and Bamberger 1994, p. 301).

Records and Data Files

Finally, evaluators can gather a great deal of useful information from program files and databases. These sources may provide valuable information on the program's purposes, history, and administration. Of particular importance for evaluations of training programs is that the files will probably contain preprogram data on the participants that evaluators can use to reconstruct their situation before entering the program (or to confirm their self-reported information) as part of a before and after comparison. Moreover, in contrast to most observation studies this form of data collection is *unobtrusive*, that is, the fact that an evaluation is being undertaken cannot affect the data in the files, which were presumably compiled for other reasons.

Evaluators must secure authorization to examine records and data files in advance. Sometimes this is relatively easy, but in other cases they may need to overcome confidentiality and privacy restrictions or other legal or bureaucratic impediments. Moreover, they may have to authenticate and verify the information. For example, when using databases evaluators must know how the data were collected and processed and, if possible, check their reliability (see GAO 1991a).

As with the other forms of data collection, evaluators should determine ahead of time what data they need for the evaluation. Simply rifling through files is not likely to yield much useful information. A formal collection instrument, similar to an observation guide, could prove helpful in directing data gatherers to relevant information.

8

Step 6: Analyzing and Interpreting the Data

The findings of an impact evaluation become meaningful to decisionmakers through the process of making sense out of the data collected. Making sense of information involves two steps: analyzing the results and interpreting them. Analysis is the process of bringing order to the data by organizing it into categories, patterns, and trends. Analysis takes time and requires good data management techniques; creativity; intellectual rigor; and hard, thoughtful work.

Getting Organized

Getting organized is an important first step in dealing with what is often referred to as information overload. Organizing the data will be easier if the evaluators have done a good job of designing the data collection instruments and developed a tracking system early on in the evaluation. The heart of data management is data storage and retrieval: without an adequate system, data can be miscoded, misplaced, lost. A good storage and retrieval system is critical for keeping track of what data are available and for permitting easy, flexible, and reliable use of the data—often by several members of an evaluation team—and for documenting the analysis so that it can, in principle, be verified.

Once the evaluators have finished collecting the data, they must ensure that the data are complete. Consolidating interview questionnaire responses, observations, interview notes, and information by institution, country, program, or other unit of analysis is a good idea. If possible, the evaluators should find a room that they alone can use during the analysis period. Depending on their budget, as well as on the availability of staff and equipment, copying completed data collection instruments may be useful. The originals can then be set aside for reference, while the copies can be coded, highlighted, cut, or pasted as required for the analysis.

Although it can be time-consuming, compiling information from mailed questionnaires is fairly straightforward. Responses to standardized items such as background information and multiple choice items and rating scales (which are typical in mailed questionnaires) can easily be coded and compiled manually on a blank questionnaire or directly entered into a computer. Compiling responses to open-ended questions requires considerably more time and creativity. Answers must be reproduced, categorized, referenced, and cross-referenced. This can be done by cutting and pasting answers for each question manually where no other option is available. Where a computer is available, software packages that search for key words to categorize qualitative data can be used. These software packages appeared on the market in the mid-1990s and are becoming increasingly easy to use and affordable (see Miles and Huberman 1994).

Analyzing Quantitative Data

Evaluators can use many forms of quantitative analysis to evaluate training programs. Two of the most useful are *statistical analysis* and *cost-effectiveness analysis*.

Statistical Analysis

Statistical analysis can occur at four levels: descriptive, associational, inferential, and causal (for a useful overview see GAO 1992).

Descriptive analysis is the usual starting point for quantitative analysis. Typically, this focuses on measures of central tendency and dispersion. Central tendency refers to the "average" measurement for all the cases on a given variable. Most commonly, these are the arithmetic mean (the total of the values on a given variable for all the cases divided by the number of cases), the median (the value on a variable above and below which half the cases fall), and the mode (the most common value across all the cases on the variable). Which of these is used depends in part on what kind of data are available. When the data are numerical, for example, the number of years participants have been employed by their sponsoring agencies, the mean is probably most useful; when the data imply some rank order, such as social status, the median likely would be used; and when the data are categorical, for instance, grouped by sex or nationality, the mode is appropriate.

Knowing the average is important, but just as critical is information on how widely dispersed the values are around that average. For numerical data, the simplest measure is the range, which is simply the difference between the highest and lowest values on the variable. The more interesting measure is the standard deviation, which in conjunction with the mean provides most of the information needed to describe the distribution of all the cases on a given variable. Many other measures of both central tendency and dispersion are available. Which statistics are appropriate for any particular analysis depends on a number of technical issues not covered here.

For studies of training programs, descriptive analyses might focus on whether individuals participated in certain programs, how much training they received, and how long ago the training took place.

Associational analysis involves the statistical estimation of the relationships between two or more variables. An association exists when the values on two (or more) characteristics vary in a systematic way. For example, if cases with high values on one variable also have high values on another, the two variables are deemed to be positively associated. Similarly, if the value on the second variable tends to be lower when the value on the first is higher, they are negatively associated. Many statistical measures of association exist, and again, which is appropriate depends on a number of technical factors. For numerical data, the most common measures are the correlation and regression coefficients. In terms of training programs, evaluators might be interested in any relationships between the characteristics of individuals (such as their position in an organization, the number of years of professional experience they have, and their gender) and the likelihood that they were selected to participate in the program.

Inferential analysis refers to the use of data from a sample to estimate the values of the population from which that sample was drawn. For example, evaluators can use outcome data on a representative sample of students who participated in a training program to estimate outcomes for all participants. That is, they can infer what is true of the population from what they know about the sample. Inferential statistics are based on the laws of probability, and involve the application of well-developed tests of the reliability and precision of population estimates. For example, an evaluator might wish to know whether any observed association between an individual's sex and the likelihood he or she was selected to participate in a training program that was found in a given sample of cases can be generalized to apply to the whole population (say, civil servants in a given region) from which the sample was drawn.

Causal analysis is used to test whether a program has actually had an effect. As discussed in chapter 4, the ability to reach causal conclusions depends not only on finding a statistical association between the program and the outcome and impact variables, but on the analysts' ability to establish the proper temporal sequence and to eliminate the effects of other factors. The analytical technique depends on the design used to collect data. For example, in the classic experimental design, the typical analysis consists of measuring the difference between values on the outcome or impact variable before and after the program, then subtracting out the before and after difference for the control group. Here, an evaluator might be interested in whether participants who completed a given training program carried out their work more efficiently or effectively.

Cost-Effectiveness Analysis

Valadez and Bamberger (1994, pp. 139–46) note that evaluators can use cost-effectiveness analysis to assess the relative efficiency of different programs designed to address the same need. Conducting a cost-efficiency analysis requires measuring costs and outcomes (or benefits), wherever these can be clearly defined and easily measured. The data typically come from project records.

The first step in conducting a cost-effectiveness study is to identify all the costs, even those not charged directly to the program. This is because programs often receive various forms of support from other sources, for example, other agencies, and failure to include these would artificially reduce estimated program costs. The study should also identify the organizations or individuals bearing these costs to ensure that program costs borne by nonprogram sources are not hidden. Then each cost needs to be estimated in accounting terms, and where costs are to be paid over a period of years, future costs should be discounted to present value estimates.

On the outcome side, evaluators must decide in advance what measures are appropriate for purposes of the evaluation. Sometimes only a single indicator may be needed, for example, how many individuals trained were still contributing to the sponsoring organization after some given period of time. When using multiple indicators, evaluators may have to weigh them differentially to take account of the relative importance of each outcome to the program's overall objectives. The selection of outcome measures is significant, because the value attached to different outcomes could vary enormously. Thus decisions about whether the program is worth its cost could be quite different depending on which outcomes are considered.

Once the evaluator has measured costs and outcomes, the next step is to compute the cost-effectiveness ratio, which is the average cost per unit (for example, cost per student trained) divided by the average value per unit of outcome (for example, improvements in measured job performance among trained students). This ratio can be expressed either as the cost of producing a given level of outcome (*constant effects*) or as the cost per unit of outcome (*constant cost*). Evaluators can also compare different programs or different versions of the same program to decide which offers the best relative value, provided outcome measures across the programs or versions are comparable.

Analyzing Qualitative Data

Qualitative analysis can take many forms, including *content analysis* and *case analysis* (see Patton 1990, pp. 371–459, for a thorough overview).

Content Analysis

Content analysis is used to analyze data drawn from interviews, observations, and documents (such as program descriptions, memoranda, and reports). Information from these sources has a way of taking on a life of its own As all sorts of interesting facts and opinions are generated and recorded, it is easy to stray from the original purpose of the evaluation and from the questions it sought to answer. Once evaluators have completed the first compilation of information, the next step is to develop a classification system for the data. Without classification, chaos reigns!

Several considerations will drive the classification system. Everything should be organized in terms of:

- The evaluation questions for which the information was collected

- The use to which the material will be put

- The need for cross-referencing, for example, whether distinctions between key variables such as country or institution will be important for analytical purposes and will need to be cross-referenced.

The evaluation questions and the hypothesized indicators (see chapter 3) provide a starting framework that may suggest an organizing scheme. Also, as evaluators are collecting data, patterns will start to emerge that may indicate the need for including additional classification categories. For example, they may discover that some unanticipated factors contributed to impact or the lack of it and want to cluster information related to these factors into distinct categories.

Problems with coding data consistently always arise. One approach is to have multiple coders work independently, and then to compare and discuss their results. This approach can not only improve the coding scheme by leading to more consistent categorization of the data, it also can provide new insights as team members share their different views on how to organize the data. For large projects with many coders, however, the senior members of the team will probably need to develop a highly structured coding scheme that coders can apply uniformly.

Once the data have been coded, they need to be analyzed. Traditionally, this has been a painstaking process that requires evaluators to sift among records of coded data by hand to identify any patterns. However, recent advances in computer technology have greatly eased the burden of conducting qualitative analyses. In particular, a number of ethnographic and linguistic computer programs have been developed that support analysis of qualitative information. The rapid development of these technologies makes listing specific programs in this manual impractical, but their availability provides expanded opportunities to conduct content analyses.

The analysis consists essentially of looking for patterns in the data. Initially, this might take the form of typologies, which organize the data into meaningful categories (see table 8-1 as an example). For example, a typology might be based on the attitudes participants express about having attended a training program. Some participants might have reported that they viewed the program instrumentally, as a means of improving their own performance; others might have said that they saw attending as a form of recreation that allowed them to get away from the day-to-day routine of their jobs; and still others might have indicated that they thought being sent to the course was a form of punishment meted out by their superiors.

Table 8-1. *Example of the Use of a Matrix to Record Data*

In each cell record quotations, examples, patterns, and activities.

Stages of program	Impacts			
	Policy dialogue	*Policy action*	*Budget allocation*	*Contacts*
Senior policy seminar (political levels), regional				
Senior seminar, national				
Policy analysis				

The major purpose of the typologies is descriptive, but they can also be used to provide insights into how the program worked and why. One way to do this is by constructing cross-classification matrixes that take data from two or more such typologies to construct a more complex and nuanced understanding of the data. For example, the participants' attitudes toward the class could be cross-classified with data on their levels and types of participation in the program, thereby providing clues to explain different styles of participation.

Ultimately, however, impact evaluation requires evaluators to move beyond description. This means developing constructs for program processes, outcomes, and impacts, generally following the same process of classification and categorization already described. These constructs can also be analyzed using cross-classification techniques, but the kinds of interpretations this analysis leads to differ from those for quantitative analysis. Patton (1990, p. 424) notes that in qualitative analysis "the emphasis is on illumination, understanding, and extrapolation, rather than causal determination, prediction, and generalization."

Case Analysis

Case studies are designed for in-depth study. A case study might consist of analyzing what happened in a particular class, or alternatively, each of several individuals in that class might be considered a case study. In either case, all the observational, interview, documentary, or other information can be useful in understanding what the case has to say about the program and its effects. The data are typically organized into a case record, organized by category as described earlier. From this, the evaluator writes a narrative that describes and analyzes the case materials.

Several dimensions of analysis apply to case study data (see GAO 1990), namely:

- The analysis is *iterative*. Data collection and analysis occur concurrently. This means that data are being analyzed as they become available, and this analysis in turn focuses later rounds of data collection.

- The process follows the *observe, think, test, revise* sequence, that is, as evaluators make observations, they think about explanations for the data. In turn, this leads them to consider what additional information they need either to confirm these explanations or to rule out alternatives. In other words, evaluators can use later rounds of data collection to test the proposed explanations, which will lead them to revise their interpretations.

- The concept implicit in this sequence is that evaluators will develop and test *rival explanations* through confirming and disconfirming evidence.

- The findings should be *reproducible*, meaning they can be tested with new cases or additional data.

- The analysis continues until evaluators judge the explanation to be *plausible and complete*. They reach causal conclusions once they have formulated a plausible, internally consistent interpretation.

Interpreting the Results and Drawing Conclusions

Interpreting the results of the analysis so as to draw conclusions involves attaching meaning to the analysis, explaining the patterns and trends observed, and looking for relationships and linkages between the various factors and the impacts. Involving the evaluation team in the interpretation of the data can help to develop collective understanding and a much richer interpretation of the patterns and relationships present in the data.

Interpretation of the data involves moving back and forth between what the data say and speculations about relationships, causes, reasons for the findings, and meanings given to the data. Ultimately, the users will ask team members, and perhaps a consultative group, to make a judgment on important conclusions from the findings.

As the members of the evaluation team go through the analysis process, they will begin to develop ideas about the results of the evaluation: preliminary answers to the main question, including a measure of the extent to which training and institutional development activities or programs have led to short-term outcomes and long-term impacts and notions about the contributing factors.

Reviewing these preliminary ideas with a representative sample of those who supplied the data, with some of the key stakeholders, or both groups may be useful. This would serve to (a) check the findings for accuracy, completeness, and credibility; (b) test the preliminary ideas on interpretation of the results; (c) generate ideas for workable recommendations to address the issues that come out of the evaluation; and (d) secure more commitment to the outcomes among those who will be involved in implementing the recommendations.

To facilitate meaningful involvement, data need to be arranged, ordered, and presented in a reasonable format that will allow readers to detect patterns. They may find the presentation of statistics and tables boring, especially if the evaluation involved numerous questions and many variables. One way of getting such reviewers involved is to leave some of the factors or some of the response percentages blank and asking them to guess. Another is to support quantitative findings by providing examples.

At this stage, which is known as data feedback, decisionmakers and stakeholders who are involved in this exercise must understand that any findings presented to them are preliminary. The discussion process is essential to clarify what the findings mean and what actions can be taken following the study to address the issues raised.

9

Step 7: Reporting the Results and Making Recommendations

Evaluators are usually responsible for writing the report. Before starting, they must identify their main readers and keep them in mind throughout the preparation of the report.

The Content of the Report

The point of an evaluation report is to communicate to decisionmakers what happened during the course of a program or project, why it happened, and how the results could be improved. Decisionmakers typically do not have a great deal of time to read and digest long, complex reports. Thus reports must be clear, succinct, and well-organized to maximize the likelihood that they will be used. A format something like the following can be helpful in meeting this objective:

- *Executive summary.* Many readers will need to rely on a brief statement of the report's conclusions and recommendations. This means that the report must contain an executive summary, which in a few pages (a maximum of four is a good guideline) presents the report's major highlights, including the purposes of the evaluation, the specific questions addressed, the major findings and conclusions, and the recommendations.

- *Evaluation purpose and objectives.* Early in the report a section needs to explain why the evaluation was carried out and what specific objectives or questions it addressed. Without a clear statement of what the evaluation was intended to achieve, readers will have a hard time understanding what the rest of the report is about.

- *Program or project description.* The program or project must also be described in sufficient detail that the intended audience for the report knows what is being evaluated. This does not mean that everything about the program or project should be included, only its main features.

- *Evaluation design.* A brief description of the evaluation design is needed to allow readers to assess the quality of the work. This should include information on the sampling strategy employed, how the data were collected, and the analytical techniques used. A frank discussion of the strengths and weaknesses of the design helps to build credibility. Detailed information about the sample, a copy of the questionnaire or other data collection instrument, and any technical issues pertinent to the study should be included in an annex. This way they can be made available to interested readers (such as other evaluators) without losing the attention of those mostly interested in the findings and recommendations.

- *Analysis and findings.* With the groundwork properly laid, the report now can turn to a presentation and analysis of the data, which will lead to a statement of the study's findings and conclusions. This is the heart of the report, in the sense that it lays out the evidence for any conclusions and recommendations the evaluators may have reached. This section needs to be clear and orderly. It should present data on each evaluation objective or question in turn to ensure that readers can understand what the data are intended to show.

- *Conclusions and recommendations.* Finally, the report should lay out the conclusions the evaluators reached and any recommendations they make. If the previous sections of the report have been written clearly, this section should present no surprises for the reader. One way to test whether the report meets this goal is to work backward from the conclusions and the recommendations by asking the following questions: What findings would be needed to reach these conclusions and recommendations, and were those in fact the findings? If so, what data would be needed to support those findings and were they presented? What would we need to know to be sure the data are valid and reliable, and does the report provide that information? Are the data appropriate for addressing the original objectives or questions that motivated the evaluation? In other words, if the recommendations can be tracked back through all the stages of the evaluation to the underlying issues, readers will probably be able to follow the report and it will likely be more persuasive.

For an alternative format specifically developed to report on the evaluation of training programs, see appendix V.

Formulating Recommendations

Recommendations are often the most visible part of the impact evaluation report. Many of the readers who have not gone through the impact evaluation process as part of the evaluation team or consultative group, especially an organization's senior executives, may limit their reading of an impact evaluation to the executive summary and recommendations. Well-written, well-derived conclusions and recommendations can work as catalysts to stimulate decisionmaking and organizational improvement. When poorly done, recommendations can leave decisionmakers and stakeholders with a sense of unfinished work, and perhaps also with the frustration of having to explain why these recommendations just cannot be implemented.

According to Patton (1982), recommendations are "suggested courses of action, proposed changes in the program or things to be maintained as they are in the program (because they work), and advice to funding agencies, program administrators, staff and others on how to improve the program based on findings and conclusions."

Two of the most important complaints about some training program evaluations is that the recommendations are impractical and that they seem to come out of nowhere, that is, they do not seem to have been derived from the data. Indeed, recommendations often appear as though they have been produced as an afterthought, or just because they are supposed to be there.

Practical recommendations that can be implemented flow naturally from decisionmakers involved in the analysis and interpretation of the data. If decisionmakers have not been involved in the complete analysis and interpretation stages of the evaluation, presenting preliminary findings and conclusions and discussing recommendations with them prior to finalizing the report is essential.

Having said this, however, we must note that long and indiscriminate lists of recommendations are not only boring, but dilute the focus on and power of the most important recommendations. Some possible ways to formulate and organize recommendations are:

- Separating recommendations that can be implemented in the relatively short term and those aimed at long-term development of the program. Decisionmakers usually take long-term recommendations more seriously when they identify some intermediate steps toward the long-term objective.

- Orienting recommendations toward funding agencies, program implementors, training officers, and so on.

> *The impact evaluation report for the EDI-FASID program was a fifty-page document that contained detailed analysis of the evaluators' conclusions and recommendations.*
>
> *The evaluators first presented a summary of their conclusions on*
> - *The short-term effectiveness and long-term impact of the six courses in the program*
> - *Their organization, content, and administration*
> - *The precourse and follow-up activities*
> - *The development of FASID as an agency for international training and its collaboration with EDI.*
>
> *This was followed by a set of ten long-term and short-term recommendations about modifications in the structure of the courses—both formulation and administration—and in the future collaborative efforts between FASID and EDI.*
>
> *The main text documented the quantitative and qualitative analyses the evaluators used to reach their conclusions and the practical recommendations that resulted from their assessment.*

- Specifying clearly which are the primary recommendations, that is, those that are strongly supported by the data and have solid support from the evaluators and the team. Recommendations that are less directly supported by the data but may be supported by the evaluators and some members of the consultative team can be identified as secondary recommendations.

No matter how the recommendations are organized, they should be written as single statements that clearly spell out what is being called for.

Formulating useful recommendations is not just a matter of clarity. It is also a matter of empathy with decisionmakers. As the saying puts it: "Don't judge a person until you've walked a mile in his shoes." Through collaborative impact evaluation, evaluators get a good sense of the complexities of the institutional development processes into which the training programs may feed and of the context in which decisionmakers operate. That can go a long way toward coming up with recommendations that are implementable.

Finally, writing recommendations is a matter of responsibility. As mentioned previously, the written word endures and can serve to help or hinder decisionmakers. Evaluators have a responsibility to write thoughtful and feasible recommendations.

Impact evaluation can be a great learning opportunity for members of an organization. It can also yield valuable feedback on training and institutional development programs. Coming to the end of an impact evaluation means having acquired information and insights to start the training cycle again, perhaps with the benefit of a little more collective wisdom.

References

Brewer, John, and Albert Hunter. 1989. *Multi-Method Research: A Synthesis of Styles.* Newbury Park, California: Sage Library of Social Research.

Carmines, Edward J., and Richard A. Zeller. 1979. *Reliability and Validity Assessments.* London: Sage.

Cook, Thomas D., and Donald T. Campbell. 1979. *Quasi-Experimentation: Design and Analysis Issues for Field Settings.* Chicago: Rand McNally.

Kirk, Jerome, and Marc Miller. 1986. *Reliability and Validity in Qualitative Research.* London: Sage.

Kirkpatrick, Donald L. 1975. *Evaluating Training Programs.* Madison, Wisconsin: American Society for Training and Development.

Kumar, Krishna. 1993. *Rapid Appraisal Methods.* Washington, D.C.: World Bank.

Lithwick, N. H. 1990. *Impact Evaluation Methodology, with Application to the Work of the EDI of the World Bank in Infrastructure and Urban Development in Sub-Saharan Africa.* Ottawa, Canada: Carleton University.

Miles, Matthew B., and A. Michael Huberman. 1994. *Qualitative Data Analysis.* Thousand Oaks, California: Sage.

Newman, John, Laura Rawlings, and Paul Gertler. 1994. "Using Randomized Control Designs in Evaluating Social Sector Programs in Developing Countries." *The World Bank Research Observer* 9 (July):181–201.

Patton, Michael Q. 1982. *Practical Evaluation.* Beverly Hills, California: Sage.

_____. 1990. "Designing Qualitative Studies." In *Qualitative Evaluation and Research Methods.* Newbury Park, California: Sage.

Pedhazur, E. J., and S. L. Pedhazur. 1991. *Measurement Design and Analysis: An Integrated Approach.* Hillsdale, New Jersey: Lawrence Elbaum Publishers.

Rist, Ray. 1989. "On the Application of Program Evaluation Designs: Sorting Out Their Use and Abuse." *Knowledge in Society* 2(4):74–96.

_____. 1994. "Influencing the Policy Process with Qualitative Research." In N. Denzin and Y. Lincoln, eds., *Handbook of Qualitative Research.* Thousand Oaks, California: Sage Publications.

Rossi, Peter H., and Howard E. Freeman. 1993. *Evaluation: A Systematic Approach.* Newbury Park, California: Sage.

GAO (U.S. General Accounting Office). 1990. *Case Study Evaluations.* Washington, D.C.

_____. 1991a. "Designing Evaluations." Washington, D.C.

_____. 1991b. "Quantitative Data Analysis: An Introduction." Washington, D.C.

_____. 1991c. "Using Structured Interviewing Techniques." Washington, D.C.

_____. 1992. *Using Statistical Sampling.* Washington, D.C.

_____. 1994. *Program Evaluation.* Washington, D.C.: Training Institute.

USAID (U.S. Agency for International Development), Africa Bureau. 1991. *A Training Impact Evaluation Methodology and Initial Operational Guide.* Washington, D.C.: Creative Associates International.

Valadez, Joseph, and Michael Bamberger, eds. 1994. *Monitoring and Evaluating Social Programs in Developing Countries: A Handbook for Policymakers, Managers, and Researchers.* Washington, D.C.: EDI.

Appendix I

Annotated Bibliography

While the literature on impact evaluation of training is limited, a substantial body of literature is available on training evaluation and field research methodologies, and on impact evaluation of projects in many diverse areas. This bibliography reviews articles, books, and documents that may be of particular relevance to those who wish to carry out impact evaluations of training and institutional development programs. It also identifies titles that provide extensive and detailed bibliographies in particular areas of interest.

Books and articles on evaluation methods and, more specifically, on impact evaluation, are presented first. Several documents produced by donor agencies and their partner institutions are reviewed later.

Brewer, John, and Albert Hunter. 1989. *Multi-Method Research: A Synthesis of Styles*. Newbury Park, California: Sage Library of Social Research.

An useful book for readers interested in triangulation, the use of multiple methods in the course of research. Methods are compared and contrasted. The authors discuss the many aspects of multi-method research approaches: the formulation of research problems, data collection, sampling and generalization, measurement, reliability and validity, hypothesis testing and causal analysis, and writing and publicizing results.

Fowler, Floyd J. 1993. *Survey Research Methods,* 2nd ed. *Applied Social Research Methods Series*, vol. 1. Newbury Park, California: Sage.

A book about standards and practical procedures for surveys designed to provide statistical descriptions of people by asking questions, usually of a sample. Surveys involve sampling, question design, and interviewing methodologies. Those who want to collect, analyze, or read about survey data will learn how details of each aspect of a survey can affect its precision, accuracy, and credibility.

Holt, Margaret E., and Bradley C. Courtenay. 1995. "An Examination of Impact Evaluations." *Continuum* 9(1):23–35.

Presents guidelines for determining whether an impact study is desirable or feasible for evaluating continuing education programs. Describes evaluation methods and program aspects that can be measured.

Jorgensen, Danny L. 1989. *Participant Observation: A Methodology for Human Studies*. Applied Social Research Methods Series, vol. 15. Newbury Park, California: Sage.

Deals effectively with defining the use and process of participant observation; developing and sustaining field relationships; observing and gathering information; recording, analyzing, coding, and sorting techniques.

Lofland, John, and Lyn H. Lofland. 1984. *Analyzing Social Settings: A Guide to Qualitative Observation and Analysis*. Belmont, California: Wadsworth Publishing.

While the topic of this book is not evaluation, it provides tips on the use of qualitative methods in gathering data (mainly observation and interviews), on analyzing the masses of data, and on writing reports. In addition to simple guidelines on the above topics, the book contains helpful suggestions on how to get along with respondents, how to collect and log information, and how to ask thoughtful questions and remain interesting. Finally, the book discusses extensively the issues of confidentiality and ethics in carrying out field studies such as evaluations.

Miles, Matthew B., and Michael Huberman. 1994. *Qualitative Data Analysis,* 2nd ed. Newbury Park, California: Sage.

An appendix (p. 311) introduces readers to computer programs for qualitative data analysis. Suggestions for use are included, as well as a summary table that lists the characteristics of about twenty software programs, including the various computer operating systems they can work with, their user friendliness, and their relative capacity in terms of coding, development of matrices, and so on.

Patton, Michael Q. 1980. *How to Use Qualitative Methods in Evaluation.* Newbury Park, California: Sage.

Michael Quinn Patton's first book on qualitative methods, which deals with the various stages of qualitative research, is now a classic. It is part of a series of books on evaluation, the *Program Evaluation Kit* by Joan L. Herman, published by the Centre for the Study of Evaluation, University of California at Los Angeles. The *Program Evaluation Kit* consists of nine books: *Evaluator's Handbook, How to Design a Program Evaluation, How to Use Qualitative Methods in Evaluation, How to Assess Program Implementation, How to Measure Attitudes, How to Measure Performance and Use Tests, How to Analyze Data, How to Communicate Evaluation Findings.*

Patton, Michael Q. 1982. *Practical Evaluation.* Beverly Hills, California: Sage.

An excellent book on evaluation practice that links evaluation research to social action in a process that is rigorous, participatory, and constantly focused on what is practical from the standpoint of the policy and the decisionmakers. Written in layman's language, the book describes a practitioner's answer to implementing the ideals of evaluation and making them practical and relevant to decisionmakers. While it does not deal precisely with impact evaluation, the general approaches to evaluation and methodology are applicable. Chapter 3 offers interesting insights on working with groups when carrying out evaluations. Part III of the book provides valuable suggestions and guidelines on selecting methodologies, developing data gathering instruments, analyzing data, and developing recommendations.

Patton, Michael Q. 1986. *Utilization-Focused Evaluation.* Newbury Park, California: Sage.

An excellent book whose main focus is to improve the usefulness of evaluations and the utilization of their results. Chapter 4 deals with focusing the evaluation. Chapter 7 covers, in more depth than the current manual, the idea of a theory of action to help with conceptualizing causal linkages. Chapter 10, on the meaning of evaluation data, provides interesting insights on analyzing, interpreting, and reporting data.

Patton, Michael Q. 1990. "Designing Qualitative Studies." In *Qualitative Evaluation and Research Methods.* Newbury Park, California: Sage.

Chapter 5, on designing qualitative studies, has a particularly useful section on case sampling (pp. 145–98). It also contains a handy chart that distinguishes between the different types of evaluations (summative, formative, and so on).

Pedhazur, E. J., and S. L. Pedhazur. 1991. *Measurement Design and Analysis: An Integrated Approach.* Hillsdale, New Jersey: Lawrence Elbaum.

Chapter 15, "Introduction to Sampling," reviews representative sampling techniques as they relate to quantitative approaches.

Punch, Maurice. 1986. *The Politics and Ethics of Fieldwork.* Newbury Park, California: Sage.

Deals with ethical considerations in fieldwork (pp. 29–48), a subject that is becoming increasingly important.

Rossi, Peter. H., and Howard E. Freeman. 1979 and 1993. *Evaluation: A Systematic Approach.* Newbury Park, California: Sage.

This is one of the few well written and fairly comprehensive books on impact evaluation of public policy programs. The technical part of the book deals more with cost-benefit evaluation and impact evaluation of public programs in the social sector. Nevertheless, the general principles apply. The last chapter on the social context of evaluation is particularly enlightening. It goes beyond technique to focus on the realities of providing input into ongoing social processes through impact evaluation and the consequences.

Yin, Robert K. 1989. *Case Study Research, Design and Methods.* Applied Social Research Methods Series, vol. 5. Newbury Park, California: Sage.

An excellent book on designing case studies, preparing for data collection, collecting and analyzing data, and composing case study reports.

Documents Written by Donor Agencies and Partner Institutions
BANQUE AFRICAINE DE DÉVELOPPEMENT (AFRICAN DEVELOPMENT BANK)

Kouassi, Bernard. *Suivi et Evaluation des Programmes de Formation: Algérie-Burundi-RCA-Chad. Rapport de Synthèse.* Abidjan, Côte d'Ivoire.

The African Development Bank's Training Centre (Centre de Formation de la Banque Africaine de Développement) commissioned this evaluation, whose objectives were to (a) evaluate the effectiveness and relevance of the training, (b) identify the impact of the bank's training on the professional performance of participants, (c) collect information on the training needs of former and future participants and of their institutions, (d) initiate a dialogue with participants and beneficiary institutions as a basis for ongoing communication with beneficiaries, (e) review and improve the implementation of action plans, and (f) recommend new directions (both content and approach) for the future.

A team of consultants agreed on the methodology to adopt, which included developing questionnaires to be administered to former participants, people in leadership positions in the institutions, and individuals responsible for economic policies. Members of each group also completed a rated questionnaire, thus providing quantitative data. The interpretation of the findings and their implications were discussed in focus groups led by the consultants. The document describes the evaluation process and methodology, and includes a copy of the questionnaires administered to the three groups.

ECONOMIC DEVELOPMENT INSTITUTE (EDI) OF THE WORLD BANK

Lithwick, N. H. 1990. *Impact Evaluation Methodology, with Application to the Work of the EDI of the World Bank in Infrastructure and Urban Development in Sub-Saharan Africa.* Ottawa, Canada: Carleton University.

This document combines a conceptual and operational framework for impact evaluation of management and senior policy seminars on policy development and institution building. In his consideration of policy impacts, the author identifies three distinct, but highly interdependent, levels of impact: on policy (consequences and processes), on policy actions (innovation and management), and on policymakers (senior officials and middle-level managers). Measures of performance at each level are set out, as are measures of inputs by EDI.

The author analyzes different methods of surveying for each level of impact and introduces sampling considerations. A similar approach is taken for institution building, where the author reviews the steps in institution building and corresponding performance indicators. General guidelines on survey instruments, interviews and questionnaires, are presented. The author concludes part I by calling for an integrated approach to impact evaluation, linking it with and feeding into the overall policy articulation cycle so as to identify the gaps in the cycle and guide future planning. Part II of the document describes application of the framework to the evaluation of EDI infrastructure training programs in Sub-Saharan Africa.

INSTITUTO INTERAMERICANO DE COOPERACIÓN PARA LA AGRICULTURA (INTER-AMERICAN INSTITUTE FOR COOPERATION IN AGRICULTURE)

Sepulveda, Sergio. 1993. *Elementos para el diseño de un sistema de sequimiento y evaluación de programas de capacitación para el desarrollo rural.* San José, Costa Rica.

This document outlines a framework for the design of a follow-up and evaluation system of the institute's institutional development activities and programs in rural development. The capacity development and participatory nature of the programs are such that the follow-up and evaluation approaches must also be participatory, starting from a joint diagnosis of training and institutional development needs that leads to a precise identification of the training and institutional development strategy.

The document makes a clear distinction between follow-up and evaluation. The proposed system of participatory follow-up is designed to provide information to decisionmaking bodies on the effectiveness and efficiency of the activities undertaken within a given period so as to allow them to identify problems; redefine priorities; reprogram activities; or adjust the technical, administrative, or financial aspects of the programs or activities. The evaluation system is meant to assess ex post the success of the activities or programs in terms of the extent to which the institutions have developed their human resources capacity; have either increased their access to or developed productive techniques; and have improved their methods, availability of training materials, and so on.

The document suggests that the impact of institutional development programs should be assessed in terms of the effectiveness of the programs' strategy in meeting institutions' needs and of the programs' outcomes in consolidating institutions' management and technical competencies, and the programs' impact on increasing institutions' analytical capacity to identify problems, determine priorities, formulate and manage productive projects effectively, and respond effectively to the needs of its constituency. The document proposes that impact evaluation be carried out by a multidisciplinary team of professionals that reviews all available documentation (including a detailed database on needs assessments and activities that is fed by a constant feedback and monitoring system), carries out extensive interviews, and holds working groups with program coordinators and institutional contacts at all levels, beneficiaries, and external consultants participating in the programs.

UNITED NATIONS DEVELOPMENT PROGRAMME (UNDP) AND WORLD BANK

UNDP and World Bank Water and Sanitation Program. 1990. *Workshop on Goals and Indicators for Monitoring and Evaluation for Water Supply and Sanitation,* June 25–29. Geneva.

This publication is one of many that came out of a series of workshops that eventually led to the publication of World Bank Technical Paper No. 207 (discussed later). This particular paper will be of interest to those working in the water and sanitation sector as it outlines a series of indicators for water and sanitation projects. It will also be of interest to those who would like to organize workshops as one means of bringing together a number of stakeholders in a program to determine the indicators. The publication provides an insightful discussion of the advantages and difficulties of such a process.

U.S. AGENCY FOR INTERNATIONAL DEVELOPMENT (USAID)

USAID Africa Bureau. 1991. *A Training Impact Evaluation Methodology and Initial Operational Guide.* Washington, D.C.: Creative Associates International.

This elaborate document outlines a theoretical and conceptual framework for an impact evaluation and defines a set of impact indicators, with particular application to scholarship programs for institutional development. The document reviews different evaluation models and examines their relevance and utility for measuring or estimating the impact of training on development. It also explores the conceptual and theoretical links between project or program design, the specific theory of induced change (that is, development, be it at the national, sectoral, institutional, or individual level), and evaluation. Changes that constitute development impact are defined, as are the characteristics, reasonable expectations, and limitations of impact evaluation.

The document identifies effectiveness and development impact as two levels of evaluation that merit consideration and introduce the concept of impact leverage, which presupposes that a single, simple solution can bring about widespread and profound changes. The document suggests that a participative approach spreading throughout the training and institution building processes, from planning for the training to evaluation, that is, a consultative process involving the trainees, the host country government, future employers, the donors, and the implementing agency is more likely to yield positive impacts.

While the document provides a list of possible indicators to be considered at the national, sectoral, organizational, and individual trainee level, it argues that situation-specific indicators formulated preferably at the planning stage by all the parties concerned are more likely to yield valid, reliable, and accurate measurement of development change than macro-level indicators. The document includes an extensive bibliography.

WORLD BANK

Narayan, Deepa. 1993. *Participatory Evaluation: Tools for Managing Change in Water and Sanitation.* World Bank Technical Paper No. 207. Washington, D.C.

This publication was written to help policymakers, managers, and planning and evaluation staff design monitoring and evaluation activities in the water and sanitation sector. Specifically, it seeks to equip those who are managing community drinking water and sanitation programs in poor communities with simple, short-cut methods they can use to foster and encourage participation while working with communities. The publication presents a framework of indicators that have been developed to guide evaluations of water and sanitation projects. In addition, the publication outlines the distinctions between participatory evaluation as a collaborative process of problem solving versus the conventional evaluation approach. It provides useful insights on how to work with outside evaluators, how to keep methods simple, and so on.

Appendix II

Evaluation of the EDI-FASID Program and Its First Six Activities

<u>**DRAFT**</u>

<u>Estimates of Work, Time and Money Required</u>

<u>Proposals for the Work</u>

1 Two external consultants will be engaged, one from Japan, the second from other sources.

2 All concerned FASID personnel and accessible Japanese resource persons will be interviewed in Japan by the first consultant.

3 All concerned EDI personnel and accessible resource persons will be interviewed in or from Washington by the second consultant.

4 The two consultants will meet in Tokyo to plan how to obtain information from three sub-samples of participants: [1] those to be interviewed personally in Japan, India, Pakistan, and the Philippines (countries where six or more participants are located); [2] those to be interviewed by a research assistant by telephone from Washington; and [3] those to complete questionnaires only. The consultants will design the necessary instruments for the sub-samples.

5 EDI will assist them in arranging for the telephone interviews and questionnaires to be handled in Washington by a research assistant; and for the participants to be interviewed in India, Pakistan, and the Philippines to be contacted in good time.

6 After meeting in Tokyo, the consultants will interview a sample of 20 Japanese participants in the city or its immediate neighborhood.

7 They will then separately visit the 3 countries (India, Pakistan, the Philippines) from which the largest numbers of participants came, and will interview all the participants who can be readily located.

8 The consultants will process the data from the interviews and questionnaires and complete their report in Washington.

Working Days Required

9   The table below sets out the activities expected of the review and the working time they are estimated to require.

Activity	Working days	Persons (number)	Staff days

Phase 1: Japanese consultant with FASID
and Japanese resource persons; study documentation
Second consultant with EDI and Washington resource
persons; study documentation; contact participants
in India, Pakistan, and the Philippines for interview.

Activity	Working days	Persons (number)	Staff days

Phase 2: Consultants meet in Tokyo to design
instruments for 3 subsamples of participants

Phase 3: a. Interviews with Japanese
participants [sample of 20]
b. Research assistant in EDI mails questionnaires
 and contacts telephone interviews.

Phase 4: Interviews in 3 countries
India, Pakistan, the Philippines

Phase 5: Processing data from interviews
 and questionnaires, and completing report

TOTAL

Timetable

10   As the work will absorb — working days, the review and assessment will require about — calendar months.

Budget

11	Budget Item	$
a.	Consultant fees	
b.	2 consultants' international travel	
c.	2 consultant subsistence	
d.	Staff assistance with telephone interviews, etc.	
e.	Contingencies	

TOTAL $

*****NOTE:** The basis for this figure is attached.

****NOTE: $— represents c. —% of the $ spent on the 6 activities.**

Possible schedule of interviews in India, Pakistan, and the Philippines

Country	Participants	Days	Travel
India (1 consultant)	15		
Pakistan (1 consultant)	14		
Philippines (1 consultant)	13		
TOTAL	**42**		

Total days required for interviewing and travel =

Appendix **III**

Municipal Development Programme for Sub-Saharan Africa Eastern and Southern Africa Module: Mid-Term Evaluation Framework and Terms of Reference

1.   Background to the Municipal Development Programme for Sub-Saharan Africa

The Municipal Development Programme (MDP) for Sub-Saharan Africa is a regional facility which seeks to analyze and improve the policy framework for enhancing the effectiveness of urban local government and expand the related human resource capabilities to do so.

The goals of the MDP, as set out in the Programme Document are to:

1.   build an analytic capacity and coordinated policy framework to introduce appropriate institutional structures for strengthening municipal governance;
2.   enhance the capabilities of municipal governments to run their operations effectively through training and effective associations of local governments;
3.   foster municipal development and build consistency within countries, the region, and among development agencies; and
4.   provide a framework for improved coordination and synergies among African participating institutions and external development agencies who work in the area of urban governance.

Activities MDP supports are:

1.   **policy studies and policy advocacy** including investigations on key decentralization issues and local/municipal governance topics in Sub-Saharan Africa;
2.   **training activities** such as policy seminars, training of trainers, support to training institutions in municipal development, and support to the formulation of training strategies at the national and regional levels;
3.   **support to municipalities** including country-specific activities such as municipal sector reviews, identification and preparation projects for decentralized cooperation, investment opportunities and promotion of community participation in municipal government at the local level, and development of guidelines for appropriate practices; and,
4.   **strengthening associations of local authorities.**

The MDP was also expected to support activities defined jointly with the Urban Management Programme.

The MDP is meant to be a flexible programme responsive to Sub-Saharan Africa needs and priorities. It was designed to build capacity of African institutions through its activities, using existing African institutions and resources wherever possible. It is managed from two regional offices in Africa, one for West Africa and one for Eastern and Southern Africa.

The MDP Eastern and Southern Africa Module was established in May 1991 as a joint undertaking of the World Bank, the Government of Italy, the International Development Research Center (IDRC) and Federation of Canadian Municipalities (FCM) of Canada, other donor development agencies, and participating African Institutions. These donor agencies have established trust funds, administered by the World Bank as the executing agency.

The MDP Eastern and Southern Africa Module is managed by a Programme Unit based in Harare. In addition to their financial contributions, donor agencies have established a Technical Support Network (TSN) consisting of specialist staff who are available as an additional resource to support and complement the Program Unit.

The Steering Committee (SC), consisting of African experts and representatives of donors, oversees the program. In addition to providing policy direction, the Steering Committee reviews and approves activities to be carried out by MDP Programme Unit and monitors the management of the programme. The Regional Director of the Programme Unit in Harare reports to the Steering Committee.

Details of the Programme goals, activities, and structure are outlined in the Programme Document for the Eastern and Southern Africa issued in Harare, May 1991.

2.   Reasons for the Evaluation

The MDP Eastern and Southern Africa Module was established in 1991 and funding was secured for an initial three-year period. By November 1992, it will have been operational for 18 months, thus half way through its first 3 years of activity. While still remaining true to the general objectives, principles, and parameters set out in the Programme document, the programme strategy adopted in Eastern and Southern Africa, the approach, specific objectives, activities, and structures have evolved since the Document was written.

The purpose of the midterm evaluation is to:
1.   assess the effectiveness of the Programme in meeting its stated objectives (have we done the right thing and have we achieved what we intended?)
2.   assess the efficiency of the Management and Advisory Structures in managing the programme (are we doing it efficiently?)
3.   determine the impacts and effects of MDP activities on African participating institutions and donor agencies (what results?)
4.   institutionalize the learning gained from the Programme activities and experiences by providing a written record (what have we learned about development and capacity building, and about how donors relate to institutions in operational terms?)

The midterm evaluation is expected to be forward-looking, i.e., it is expected to synthesize findings on both outputs and process, and to draw lessons to inform planning of actions and activities to be undertaken by MDP in the second half of its first three year mandate.

3.   Intended Outcomes and Indicators to be Evaluated

The MDP Eastern and Southern Africa Module is working towards meeting the objectives outlined in the Programme Document and summarized in section 1. As stated in section 2, the midterm evaluation will assess the entire MDP system, including MDP activities and their impact, as well as effectiveness of management and advisory structures including the SC, AFTIN as the Executing Agency, the PU and the TSN. Intended outcomes, quantitative and qualitative indicators of success towards which MDP is striving, have been identified and are summarized in Annex 1. Given the large number of possible indicators, the SC will identify priorities for data collection and analysis.

4. Clients of the Evaluation: Authority and Responsibility

The clients of the midterm evaluation are the members of the Steering Committee. For development and implementation of the evaluation, the consultant will report to the EDI Task Manager for the MDP who will manage the evaluation on behalf of the Steering Committee. The draft evaluation report will be presented to the members of the Steering Committee.

5. The Evaluation Approach

A number of written sources of information are available to the evaluator. These include:

1. Reports compiled by the Programme Unit documenting activities (objectives, target audience, expected outcomes, process, and actual outcomes) completed following each activity;
2. Activity completion and progress reports written by the Participating Institutions (where they have been submitted), describing their perceptions of MDP's and their own contributions, and documenting their evaluation of effectiveness, efficiency, and impact of the activities;
3. Reports to the Steering Committee, including regular updates on activity processes and outcomes, and information on the management of the programme;
4. Background documentation including the Operation Manual, Guidelines for User Participation, and the two Business Plans (May 1992 and November 1991);
5. Other documents, including letters and reports documenting donor/MDP and MDP/participating institution interaction.

While some of the expected outcomes are documented and quantifiable, qualitative indicators and processes can only be explored through in-depth open-ended interviews. Thus, where possible, the preferred approach will be the personal interview in the field location.

In addition to reviewing existing documentation, the evaluator will be expected to gather data on effectiveness, efficiency, and impact through interviews with:

1. **MDP's clients/beneficiaries:** the participating institutions which have been the direct beneficiaries including some local government training institutions, some central governments and some local authorities. Participants to the MDP activities should be surveyed. Third parties who may provide some measure of validation should also be surveyed: these could include participants' immediate supervisors, the institutional leadership, and/or relevant actors in Central Government.

2. **Various actors in the MDP:** members of the Steering Committee, including the African members and donor representatives; members of the Technical Support Network; those who are tasked with managing the Programme including the representatives of the Executing Agency in Washington and of Resident Missions in the various African countries where MDP has held activities, the Regional Director and staff of the Programme Unit in Harare; consultants and resource persons who have been involved in MDP activities to date.

Within the general guidelines outlined above, the evaluator will be expected to prepare an evaluation methodology, to develop data collection instruments and prepare an evaluation workplan to be submitted to the MDP.

6. Statement of Qualifications for the Consultant

MDP proposes to retain the services of an African consultant with the following qualifications:

- graduate level academic qualifications in urban planning and management, public administration, and/or human resource development;

- demonstrated experience in evaluating training and institutional development and/or capacity building projects in the public sector in Africa, preferably in local government;

- knowledge and understanding of local government challenges, issues and institutions in Eastern and Southern Africa;

- excellent oral and written communication skills.

The evaluation consultant will be expected to:

- clarify the Terms of Reference

- prepare a workplan for the evaluation and revise it as required

- develop data collection instruments and collect data with appropriate sensitivity to MDP's needs and its role in participating institutions

- maintain the highest ethical standard throughout

- prepare a draft report for presentation to the Steering Committee

- prepare a revised report following comments

- perform the evaluation in a timely manner, as agreed.

Appendix IV

Example of a Survey Questionnaire

China Network for Training and Research
in Health Economics and Financing

Survey Questionnaire (original English version)

Guidelines for completing this survey

You may recall that you attended a seminar on public health economics and financing organized by the Network for Training and Research in Health Economics and Financing with support from the Ministry of Public Health and the World Bank. Seminars such as the one you attended were designed to introduce high level officials responsible for policy formulation and implementation to options and alternatives for a more effective public health system and to facilitate exchange of views and experience with Chinese and foreign experts.

As part of the Network's efforts to be effective and responsive to needs in the public health sector in China, the Economic Development Institute (EDI) of the World Bank is sponsoring an external follow-up study to determine the impact of the seminar(s) you attended.

The attached questionnaire has been developed to find out what former seminar participants hoped to apply to their work after the seminar, what actions they were able to take, and what constraints they face. EDI and the Chinese Network for Training and Research in Health Economics and Financing are particularly interested in your views and suggestions on how the Network could better meet your needs in the future. You may also be contacted by one of two Chinese collaborators in the evaluation team who will carry out interviews with a selected number of former seminar participants in China. We would be most grateful for your collaboration.

Please note that the study is not seeking any personal information from you, nor is the purpose of this study to evaluate seminar participants or their agencies. Only trends will be reported and your observations will be kept strictly confidential.

I would be most grateful if you could complete the attached questionnaire as soon as you receive it and return it in the enclosed stamped envelope so that it can be received in Shanghai before the October 15 deadline. Thank you for your kind assistance.

Suzanne Taschereau
McGill University
Montreal, Canada

Survey of Senior Seminar Participants

GENERAL INFORMATION (for statistical purposes only)

Your Province: ....

Please circle the <u>letter</u> beside the answer you consider most accurate.

1.   The Senior Policy Seminar you attended:

a)   Health Financing   Shanghai, May 27–June 1, 1991

b)   Financing and Resource Utilization of
      Health Care in Rural Areas   Chengdu, Oct. 12–17, 1992

c)   Economic Reform and the Health
      Sector under the Socialist Market Economy   Beijing, July, 29–31, 1993

2.   When you attended the course, your level of responsibility was:

a)   Vice-Governor   g)   Associate Professor
b   Director   h)   Professor
c)   Deputy Director   i)   Assistant Professor
d)   Chief   j)   Lecturer
e)   Vice-Chief   k)   Other.   Please specify:
f)   Secretary

3.   You were working in:

a)   Central Government
b)   Provincial Government
c)   Municipal Government
d)   University/training/research institute
e)   Other.   Specify:

4.   The main responsibility of your office/unit was:

a)   Public Health Administration
b)   Finance
c)   Planning
d)   Price Administration
e)   Training and Research
f)   Other.   Please specify:

5.   Your technical background when you attended the Seminar was:

a)   Public Administration
b)   Medical Doctor
c)   University education with specialized courses or seminars in public health financing
      and/or economics and/or finance
d)   Other.   Specify:

6. **Your position is now:**

   a) The same as at the time of the seminar
   b) Different with increased responsibility.   Please specify:
   c) Other.   Please give details:

BENEFITS OF THE SEMINAR

The following questions ask you to give a rating to your answer on a scale where 1 refers to "not at all" and 6 refers to "to a great extent." Please circle the <u>number</u> which represents more closely your assessment of the extent to which the answer applies. Circle N/A if the question does not apply to you.

7. To what extent do you feel the seminar you attended benefitted you through:	Not at all applicable 1	2	3	4	To a great extent 5	6	Not (N/A)
a) A better understanding of policy options for public health planning and financing	1	2	3	4	5	6	N/A
b) New knowledge and ideas on how to deal with public health management and financing issues	1	2	3	4	5	6	N/A
c) Increased confidence to discuss policy reform issues and alternatives	1	2	3	4	5	6	N/A
d) Developing and maintaining contacts and dialogue with seminar participants after returning to your work	1	2	3	4	5	6	N/A
e) Developing and maintaining contacts with experts from international institutions	1	2	3	4	5	6	N/A

8. To what extent did the following aspects or components contribute to the value of the seminar?	Not at all 1	2	3	4	5	To a great extent 6	Not applicable (N/A)
a) The ideas on health economics concepts and theories	1	2	3	4	5	6	N/A
b) Case studies prepared by Chinese universities in the Network	1	2	3	4	5	6	N/A
c) Having participants from different government departments	1	2	3	4	5	6	N/A

d) Having more than one participant
from your province and/or ministry
attending Network seminars
in health economics and finance,
thereby increasing the potential
of future support and cooperation 1   2   3   4   5   6   N/A

e) Presentations and lectures by
Chinese lecturers and
researchers from the Network   1   2   3   4   5   6   N/A

f) Presentations and lectures by
foreign experts   1   2   3   4   5   6   N/A

9. Have you been able to share ideas and knowledge gained from the seminar?
Please circle "Yes" or "No" next to each statement.

a) Through discussing new ideas with your superior(s) and colleagues   Yes   No

b) Representations made to policy fora or to policy implementing
bodies at higher levels   Yes   No

c) Formal presentations made to your unit or others   Yes   No

d) Ideas debated in your unit for implementation at the
provincial level   Yes   No

e) Distribution of seminar materials   Yes   No

f) Organizing and/or giving courses/seminars/workshops   Yes   No

Please give some details (content, duration, and audience) ....
....
....

APPLICATION TO YOUR WORK

10. To what extent were you able to act on the following when you returned to your office?

	Not at all 1	2	3	4	5	To a great extent 6	Not applicable (N/A)
a) Formulate policy proposals for policymakers on health planning, management, and financing options and alternatives	1	2	3	4	5	6	N/A

Please specify: ....
....

b) Introduce increases in public
health budget in the rural areas   1   2   3   4   5   6   N/A

c) Allocate more resources to
    prevention and primary care   1   2   3   4   5   6   N/A

d) Experiment with a new
    approach to deal with urgent
    health financing issues
    you were facing.   1   2   3   4   5   6   N/A

Please give some details on the issue(s) you were facing, how you had dealt with them before
the seminar, and what new approach you experimented with following the seminar: ....
....
....

d) Pursue policy dialogue between
    policy makers at central and
    provincial levels of governments.   1   2   3   4   5   6   N/A

Please give examples, and specify if these are informal contacts or institutional links: ....
....
....

e) Formulate action plans for
    implementation of changes in
    the public health system so that
    it is more cost-effective   1   2   3   4   5   6   N/A

f) Experiment with new health
    financing mechanisms: employee
    health insurance, rural cooperative,
    cost sharing, etc.   1   2   3   4   5   6   N/A

Please give details: ....
....
....

11. Please give specific examples of how you have used information from the seminar in your job.
....
....
....
....

12. To what extent have the following been important obstacles in your attempts to influence or implement public health financing policy?	Not at all 1	2	3	4	5	To a great extent 6	Not applicable (N/A)
a) The public health financing policy alternatives and approaches were not applicable to China's circumstances	1	2	3	4	5	6	N/A
b) The policy alternatives and public health planning, management, and financing approaches were not applicable in your province/office	1	2	3	4	5	6	N/A

c)	Lack of support at higher levels	1	2	3	4	5	6	N/A

d)	Lack of funding to implement	1	2	3	4	5	6	N/A

e)	Insufficient theoretical basis and skills in your institution to plan and implement the changes	1	2	3	4	5	6	N/A

f)	You were assigned other duties	1	2	3	4	5	6	N/A

g)	Resistance from other agencies or departments whose support was necessary	1	2	3	4	5	6	N/A

h)	You would have needed more follow-up support from the Network to tailor proposed approaches to your own circumstances	1	2	3	4	5	6	N/A

i)   Other: Please specify:..
     ....
     ....

13. Since the workshop, what changes have been made to the public health planning, management, and financing systems which have had an impact on your work? ....
    ....
    ....
    ....
    ....

14. Have you maintained contact with the Network China Network for Training and Research in Health Economics and Financing and/or any of its member institutions?

If your answer is no, go directly to question 15.

If your answer is yes, please specify:

1. The nature of this contact:

    a) use of Network staff, resource persons, and consultants
    b) follow-up information request and advice
    c) request for materials and/or research reports
    d) other:

2. Whether you have maintained contact with the Network through:

    a) the coordinating institution in Beijing
    b) the training institution organizing the seminar
    c) the training institution closest to you geographically
    d) individuals you found most knowledgeable given the issues you face at your work
    e) other:

13. How could the Network increase its impact on public health planning, management, and .... financing in China? Please write your comments and suggestions. ....
....
....
....
....
....
....

****

Thank you for taking the time to complete this questionnaire.

Please put the completed questionnaire in the enclosed self-addressed stamped envelope and mail so that the questionnaire can be received in Shanghai <u>before the October 15 deadline.</u>

Appendix V

Proposed Final Training Project Evaluation Report Outline

What follows is a proposed outline that may be used in reporting the evaluation findings. The outline has ten major sections. Not every report will necessarily include each and every point for all ten sections stated below. But it is assumed that each of the ten key sections will be present and only in a rare instance would it not be addressed in the final report.

1) Title Page

2) Table of Contents

3) Executive Summary (No more than 4 pages addressing sections 4–10 listed below)

4) Introduction and Scope of Project

- TOR
- Financing arrangements
- Competitive procedures used to select beneficiary or grant recipient
- Key strengths of winning bid
- Basis for the selection of the target group for the training (professional characteristics, critical training needs to be met, etc.)
- Discussion of the needs assessment done to document demand

5) Project Design
- What are the project inputs (staffing expertise, curriculum materials, financial support, etc.)
- What are the project outputs (# of persons completing training, hours of instruction, exposure to particular substantive areas, etc.)
- What are the project outcomes (documentation of learning that occurred, new skills acquired, new concepts that have been understood, etc.)
- What are the project impacts (changes in individual behavior, changes in organizational policies, procedures, or rules, new laws, new regulations, new deregulations)

6) Training Course and Materials Preparation
- Describe how materials and course curriculum were related to needs assessment
- What existing materials were used and what new materials were developed
- Identification of experts who assisted in development of new materials (if done)
- Discussion of pilot efforts to test appropriateness of course content and materials
- Discussion of changes made after pilot phase and why

7) Project Implementation
- Discuss logistics (facilities and their quality, location, travel requirements, etc.)
- Discuss attributes of person attending course or program
- Discuss the expertise of the presenters
- Discuss the pedagogical strategies used and why:
  - lectures

- small group discussions
- field visits/study tours
- internships
- panel presentations
- use of instructional technology
- independent study
- distance learning
- others

- Discuss any modifications made to the curriculum during the course or program
- Discuss monitoring efforts made during the course or program to ensure that the training and materials were:
  - meeting stated objectives
  - understood by participants
  - challenging to participants
  - at the appropriate level of intellectual complexity

8) Project Assessment and Evaluation
- Describe the methods used to monitor and evaluate the course or program, for example:
  - end of course evaluation
  - pre and post tests on subject matter learning
  - surveys and/or questionnaires
  - focus groups
  - individual interviews
  - tracer studies of participants 3 months after the completion of the course or project
  - individual written journals
  - financial data
  - others

- Describe the criteria for determining:
  - inputs
  - outputs
  - outcomes
  - impacts
  - costs per participant by and total project

9) Project Finding and Results
- Discussion of Outputs (in relation to requirements) for example:
  - # of participants
  - # of new materials produced
  - # of hours/days of instruction
  - # of modules/topics covered

- Discussion of Outcomes, for example:
  - documented learning that took place
  - documented new skills mastered
  - documented change in attitudes or expectations

- Discussion of Impacts, for example:
  - documented changes in individual behavior
  - documented uses of new materials by individuals or organizations
  - documented changes in rules, procedures, guidelines, regulations, or practices by organization

- Discussion of the Evidence Regarding the Multiplication Principle
- Discussion of the Quality of Technical Assistance Received

- Discussion of the Costs for each participant per day and for the total project
- Discussion of the Strategies for dissemination of materials

10) Conclusions and Recommendations
- The appropriateness of the Design for this course or project
- The implementation of this course or project
- The financing of this course or project
- The use of technical expertise in this course or project
- The achievement of the learning objectives
- The achievement of the impact objectives

- Other Observations
  - project efficiency
  - cost-benefit considerations

- Lessons Learned For Future Initiatives